How Not To F*cking Hate People!

(And Maybe, Accidentally, Make the World Suck Less)

Jeffrey Alan

Sugar Leaf Media

Copyright © 2025 Jeffrey Alan

All rights reserved.

No part of this book may be reproduced or transmitted in any form or by any means, electronic or mechanical, including photocopying, recording, or by any information storage and retrieval system, without prior written permission from the publisher, except in the case of brief quotations used in reviews or articles.

Published by Sugar Leaf Media

Contents

Author's Note — 3
The First Rule of Humanity — and the One We Keep Breaking

Prologue — 7
When Outrage Divides and Kindness Heals

Chapter — 15

Introduction — 17
How Not to F*cking Hate People!

Prelude — 27
Why We F*cking Hate People!

PART ONE — 29

1. Raw Hate: Road Rage! — 31
   Primal hate on four wheels. Why tinted windows, anonymity, and ego create the perfect storm — and how humor can flip it

2. Karens and Darrens: Driving the Mothership of Hate — 37
   Modern moral policing, viral outrage, and what coconut water can teach us about emotional intelligence

3. Friends and "Frenemies" — 45
   How to Stay Kind When They Mess Up — and When You Do Too

4. The Everyday Fights — 57
   How to Stay Kind When People Suck (Just a Little...or a lot!)

5. Cancelling Cancel Culture 83
   When the World Tries to Cancel You — and You Refuse to Play Along

PART TWO 95

7. When Worldviews Collide 99
   Some knots take more than one pair of hands to untie.

8. When Hate Goes Global 113
   The New Pandemic

Afterword 127
Real people proving that courage, empathy, and humor still work — and what we can learn from them.

Epilogue — The Final Mirror 141
How to walk through madness without matching its tone.

Acknowledgements 155
The voices, hearts, and divine nudges that helped bring this book to life.

Author's Reflection 159
A deeper dive into pluralism, faith, and the radical art of coexisting.

Appendix A 163
Catching Ourselves in the Act: 25 Ways Hate Sneaks In (and How to Flip Them)

Appendix B 168
The Power of Open Dialogue

About the author 171

Written for one reason:

To stop the senseless hatred destroying our world.

Author's Note

The First Rule of Humanity — and the One We Keep Breaking

Every major faith has the same number-one rule.

In the Bible: *"Love your neighbor as yourself."*

In the Torah: *"Ve'ahavta l're'acha kamocha."* Literally " Love your neighbor as yourself."

In the Qur'an and Hadith: *"Lā yu'minu aḥadukum ḥattā yuḥibba li-akhīhi mā yuḥibbu li-nafsih."*

Transliteration: *La yu'minu ahadukum hatta yuhibba li-akhi-hi ma yuhibbu li-nafsih.*

"None of you truly believes until he loves for his brother what he loves for himself".

In the Buddhist Metta Sutta: *"Just as a mother would protect her only child with her life, even so should one cultivate boundless love toward all living beings."*

Call it a commandment, a teaching, a law, or a code — whatever word fits your faith, the idea is identical:

The point of religion was never division. It was love.

And somewhere along the way, we forgot that.

We started to confuse *different* with *dangerous*.

We stopped sitting with people who saw the world differently —

and started shouting over them instead.

That's where the ancient idea of pluralism got lost:

the belief that truth can have more than one accent,

that faith, culture, and conscience can coexist

without canceling each other out.

Pluralism is radical humility.

It says: *my truth matters — and so might yours.*

It's the muscle we've allowed to atrophy,

the one that keeps civilization intact.

The most painful places this commandment should apply

are often where it's most ignored.

Between nations, neighbors, and even families who share the same blood.

You can see it in conflicts all over the world —

from Israel and Palestine to communities at war with themselves.

People who've lived side by side for generations,

through fear and friendship, tragedy and triumph,

forgetting that the first rule of every sacred text

wasn't *who's right*, but *how we love*.

It doesn't say:

- Love your fellow Jew.
- Love your fellow Muslim.
- Love your fellow Christian.
- Love your fellow gay or straight friend.
- Love your fellow Latino, Black, or Asian neighbor.
- Love the person who votes, prays, or looks like you.

It says *neighbor*.

Which means *different*.

Which means the person across the street, across the border, across the aisle.

And that's where this book begins —

not in politics or theology,

but in the stubborn, simple question:

How do we love our neighbors again?

Not the easy ones.

The ones who cut us off in traffic.

The ones who cancel us online.

The ones who make family dinners feel like hostage negotiations.

The ones who vote the "wrong" way, pray the "wrong" way, love the "wrong" way.

Because if we can't coexist in the small ways,

how can we ever hope to do it in the big ones?

Kindness isn't weakness.

It's strategy.

It's how we practice pluralism in real time.

God didn't say it would be easy.

He said it would be necessary.

And maybe — just maybe —

if we stop treating *"Love thy neighbor"* like a bumper sticker

and start treating it like the radical, world-saving command it was meant to be —

we can begin to heal the hate that's made us all so tired.

A Note on Intermission Cards

Between some of the chapters, you'll find a little *"Intermission Card."*

They're there to give you a breather — a moment to laugh, reflect, absorb, and shift gears before diving back in.

Think of them as road signs on the highway to sanity —

small pauses to catch your breath, check your mirrors,

and remember where you're going before you hit the next stretch of chaos.

Because sometimes, the space between the stories

is where the meaning actually lands.

Kindness is free.

Prologue

When Outrage Divides and Kindness Heals

The Theater of Righteousness

Hatred doesn't always come dressed as rage. Sometimes it arrives smiling from behind a studio desk, wrapped in applause and moral certainty. It sells itself as courage — as "speaking truth to power." But what it's often selling is something much cheaper: performance.

In today's media landscape, entire shows are built around the illusion of dialogue. The panels, the interruptions, the crowd reactions — they all mimic conversation while carefully avoiding what conversation actually requires: humility, curiosity, and the risk of being changed. What we see instead are pre-written arguments dressed up as debate.

Take a recent example. A popular talk-show host publicly promised to wear a political hat — a symbol of loyalty to one camp — if the President succeeded in bringing home the hostages. When that promise went unkept, the outrage machine ignited: critics accused her of hypocrisy, fans defended her as nuanced, and the entire spectacle became another round in America's endless blame-ping-pong.

But the real story isn't the hat or the host. It's the performance of moral seriousness that collapses under the weight of its own insincerity. This isn't unique to one network or ideology. If the same thing had happened on a conservative program — a pundit making a self-righteous promise on camera and then quietly retreating — it would be just as revealing. The problem isn't who did it. The problem is that we've built an entire culture that rewards posturing over integrity.

Had she kept her word — had she actually put on that hat — she could've done something extraordinary.

She could've broken the algorithm.

For five seconds, she could've proven that empathy doesn't mean agreement.

That kindness doesn't require conversion.

That we can acknowledge good wherever it appears, even in people we don't like.

That one simple act could've built a bridge over the canyon we keep pretending is unbridgeable.

Instead, she missed the moment.

And to be fair — I've looked for examples like it on any side of the aisle.

Broken promises are everywhere in politics, but this one stands out because of the stage it happened on: live TV, daytime, with an audience applauding the setup. It wasn't vague — it was concrete.

"If he brings home hostages, I'll wear the hat."

He did.

She didn't.

And because the hat is such a visible symbol, the failure became visible too.

It wasn't whispered on social media; it was replayed across networks.

Media on both sides **amplified it** — conservatives using it as proof of hypocrisy, liberals quietly downplaying it as if silence could erase the tape.

That's what makes the moment different.

It wasn't the politics — it was the performance.

It was a televised promise, instantly measurable, followed by a silence that spoke volumes.

And here's the truth that transcends sides: progress was made. Hostages came home.

People who had been enemies for generations sat down at the same table and began the fragile, uncertain work of talking about peace.

Whether that peace lasts is anyone's guess, but the fact that the conversation even began deserved acknowledgment.

The point isn't who gets the credit. The point is what we choose to do with moments like that — whether we meet them with cynicism or with the grace to say, that was good.

Grace doesn't mean agreement.

It means recognizing that even people we dislike are capable of doing something right.

The inability to do that — to praise an opponent without feeling like we've betrayed our tribe — is exactly how the cancer of hate spreads.

It's not politicians alone who divide us.

It's the machinery built to make sure we never see each other as human again.

Every clip, every chyron, every "gotcha" headline trains us to hate by reflex.

The media profits from our outrage and programs us to feel morally superior for it.

We think we're thinking — but we're being played.

And that's why this moment matters.

Because the smallest act of integrity — one talk-show host keeping her word — could have cracked that illusion wide open.

For one day, millions of people might've seen that you can keep your word and keep your dignity.

You can disagree and still give credit where it's due.

You can love your country and love the people who see it differently.

Every time someone performs conviction without consequence, we teach audiences that sincerity is optional and accountability is negotiable. The cycle feeds itself: the audience applauds, the clip goes viral, and the next promise becomes even louder — and emptier. Soon, outrage isn't a reaction to injustice; it's a form of entertainment.

And here's where the damage runs deep. These spectacles don't just shape opinions — they shape how we feel about each other. When we see disagreement modeled as mockery, or virtue used as a weapon, we learn that contempt is the price of belonging. We stop listening. We stop believing that good faith even exists.

This is how hate grows quietly inside moral performance. Not through shouting matches or violent rhetoric, but through the slow corrosion of integrity — the sense that words no longer need to mean anything. Whether it's a daytime host or a primetime pundit, the effect is the same: people begin to distrust everyone, not just the speaker.

The lesson isn't that we should silence debate or cancel those who fail their own tests. The lesson is simpler, and harder: say what you mean, and mean what you say. The measure of moral courage isn't in the slogans we wear but in whether we keep our word when no one's clapping.

If we want to unlearn hate, we have to start by rejecting the theater of righteousness — the applause-based version of truth that rewards performance over principle. Because hate doesn't need villains to grow; it only needs insincerity.

———

When moral theater replaces moral courage, something dangerous happens — contempt starts to sound like virtue.

And that's where hate begins: not in riots or rallies, but in language that flatters our empathy while slowly poisoning it.

When Hate Begins in the Language of Virtue

Hatred rarely walks through the door calling itself hate. It enters dressed in moral language — empathy, justice, liberation — words that sound noble but often conceal contempt. The most dangerous kind of hate isn't loud or vulgar. It's intellectual. It flatters the reader into feeling morally superior while quietly training them to despise entire groups of people.

A perfect example is a recent Guardian column by a well-read journalist that claims the horrors committed in Gaza will "come home" to the West. At first glance, it reads like moral reflection.

But beneath the surface lies a poisonous idea: that "the West" — a term used so broadly it turns millions of different people into one convenient villain — has "dehumanized itself," that entire nations are collectively guilty.

How blatantly manipulative can you get? It's moral blackmail disguised as empathy — a narrative that punishes nuance and rewards outrage.

There's no effort to see the humanity of those who disagree, no curiosity about why events unfolded as they did, no invitation to understanding. It replaces dialogue with accusation, compassion with condemnation.

This is how hatred germinates — not in mobs with torches, but in essays that divide humanity into saints and sinners, victims and villains. It starts when someone claims moral ownership of suffering and turns empathy into a weapon. When writers strip complexity from human tragedy, they create emotional permission for contempt. And contempt, left unchallenged, always ripens into hate.

The lesson is simple but urgent: read between the lines. Ask why the author wrote it, what emotion they want you to feel, and who they want you to despise. Hatred often begins not with a clenched fist, but with a self-satisfied nod — when the reader says, *Yes, I am better than them.*

But while words can divide, actions can also heal. And somewhere else, six young men were proving it.

How Kindness Heals

as1one: The Hatefully Impossible Boy Band and the Third Side

They showed up in Los Angeles on October 6, 2023 — six young men bundled into a boy band called As1One: four Israelis, two Palestinians — dreaming of music, tours, microphones, harmony. They were already living together, cooking dinner, practicing choreography, forging brotherhood across the ancient divide.

Then morning came. October 7. And the messages flooded in.

A Nova music festival massacre had claimed the lives of two of the Israeli members' closest friends. Suddenly, grief wasn't theoretical — it was real. Terrifying. Intimate.

That morning, when he discovered the news about his friends, one of the Palestinian members did something extraordinary: he held him. He wrapped his arms around his brother in that band — not just as a fellow musician, but as proof that tenderness can still exist under fire.

Think about it. A young man, wrecked by loss, is held by someone he's supposed to consider the enemy. Someone whose people are being bombed even as they sit together in that quiet L.A. room. And yet, in that moment, there's no war between them. There's only grief. Human grief. Shared, wordless, gut-level grief.

No one would have blamed them if they'd broken apart right there. If hate had ripped them apart as it seems to rip everything else.

But what did they do next?

The band gathered. Not just to console — but to decide.

Because they knew what was coming. They could already hear the world sharpening its knives. Their social media would be watched. Their lyrics picked apart. Every word a landmine. Every silence, a side.

So what did they do?

They stayed together.

They didn't fracture.

They didn't post dueling statements or retreat into tribal corners.

They doubled down on love.

They kept making music.

They kept living together.

They kept showing up for each other, cooking dinner like nothing was on fire — when literally everything was.

Because they had already figured out what governments, militias, and keyboard warriors still can't:

You can hold space for someone else's pain without erasing your own.

You can lose people to a war and choose to be a different kind of soldier in it — soldiers fighting for something new. Soldiers fighting with a message of love, compassion, acceptance, and peace. Not soldiers for either side. Soldiers for the third side.

They stayed in that house. They talked. Openly. Freely.

They compromised. They listened. They sought to deeply understand each other.

They're thriving. Their debut single, All Eyes on Us — featuring Nile Rodgers — opened the door, and they've since followed with Stranger and Together As One, continuing to blend music and meaning in ways that transcend borders. Today they perform tirelessly. They tour. They've become a symbol.

Their message? Israelis and Palestinians can live together, make music together, love together — not in fantasy, but in reality and under real threat.

That moment — six voices joined across centuries of hate — is not a side note or a cute story.

It's the lighthouse in the middle of the battlefield.

Hate sells because it's easy.

Love lasts because it's work.

What those six young men remind us — what every missed promise and broken broadcast proves — is that peace isn't a miracle, it's maintenance. It's the small, stubborn act of showing up with grace when outrage would be easier.

That's how we stop hating people.

Not with speeches.

With choices.

"I Fucking Hate People!"

—Julia Roberts, *Leave the World Behind*

Introduction

How Not to F*cking Hate People!

It started with one sentence.

A customer came by my little outdoor shop one morning, clutching her coffee like it was emotional support.

She'd just gotten off the phone with an ex-friend — someone voting for Trump.

She sighed, looked up at me, and said:

"I wish I could figure out how not to hate people.

It's just so visceral, you know?"

And yeah — I knew.

Because that same week, I'd watched *Julia Roberts* in *Leave the World Behind*.

There's this scene where she's packing her family's bags on a random Tuesday morning.

Her husband wakes up to Julia packing their bags, confused:

"What are you doing?"

"We're going on vacation."

"Why... on a Tuesday?"

And she looks out the window at the world and says,

"Because I fucking hate people."

That line hit me like a slap and a mirror at the same time.

Because it wasn't cruel.

It was honest.

We've all had that Tuesday —

the one where you can't scroll, talk, or even breathe without wanting to scream into a throw pillow.

The world's too loud, too angry, too smug.

Everyone's offended, no one's listening,

and somehow it's your fault for not being *more understanding*.

That was the moment this book was born — from that space between exhaustion and hope.

Kindness is Free.

This isn't a self—help book in Vuori or Alo yoga pants.

I'm not going to tell you to breathe deeply while people stomp all over your boundaries.

This is a book for people who are done.

For people who scream at traffic lights.

For people who slam their laptops shut after one more unhinged Facebook post.

For people who've been bullied, erased, ignored, or written off —

too liberal, too conservative, too religious, too non-religious,

too much, too little, too something.

People hating each other because they voted for Donald Trump.

Or because they admired Charlie Kirk.

Or because they listened to Candace Owens.

Or because they still quote Barack Obama, voted for Joe Biden,

or believe Bernie Sanders had a plan.

Here's the kicker: the crazy isn't partisan.

Hate doesn't care what side of the aisle you sit on.

I've seen conservatives dehumanized for thinking differently,

and progressives cancel each other for not being "liberal" enough.

Different tribes, same disease — addiction to outrage, righteousness, and control.

You've seen them —

the ones dancing in the streets, cheering someone's downfall,

the ones shouting from pulpits or soapboxes,

preaching the apocalypse like it's good news.

Two flavors.

One poison.

And the media?

They're the bartenders — happily over-pouring.

CNN, Fox, MSNBC, YouTube, TikTok — it doesn't matter.

None of them are in the truth business.

They're in the eyeballs business.

And we fall for it — all of us.

The media isn't what it used to be. Or maybe it is — and we're only just figuring it out.

Outrage feels righteous, and righteousness feels safe.

They'll feed you whatever keeps you clicking, swiping, hating.

Your algorithm isn't reality — it's a fun-house mirror that shows you only what makes you mad.

My feed looks different than yours.

Yours looks different than your neighbor's.

And then we all wonder why we can't even agree on what's true anymore.

So here's the rule:

Believe in your heart — *or at least your own eyes* — before you believe a headline.

Measure humanity face-to-face before you measure it in memes.

And if you do listen to the media, take it with a dump truck of salt.

Because that's the fuel for all this hate —

a billion outrage loops convincing us that people aren't people anymore,

just avatars of everything we despise.

That's why this book exists.

It's not about kumbaya or rolling over.

It's about surviving a world on fire without becoming the arsonist.

It's about walking through madness without matching its tone.

It's about how not to fucking hate people —

and maybe, just maybe,

help them hate a little less too.

Because in the end, we all have a choice:

Hate is easy.

Kindness is Free.

Before We Get Started

So where does all this hate actually come from?

That hard-wired cortisol spike that makes us seethe —

the invisible smoke curling out of our ears,

the tightening jaw, the teeth grinding,

the "are you kidding me right now?" glare at the steering wheel.

That's not just attitude.

That's chemistry.

And it's been trained into us since birth.

We like to think hate starts with "bad people."

It doesn't.

It starts with programming.

You grow up watching your parents curse out the driver ahead of them,

your uncle dropping slurs at the dinner table,

your teacher rolling their eyes at "those people."

You soak it up before you can even spell it.

Indoctrination doesn't wear a uniform.

It wears a smile.

It sits at the breakfast table,

gets passed down like family heirlooms —

the stories, the stereotypes, the "truths" no one questions.

Because indoctrination is efficient.

It installs belief before reasoning develops.

It doesn't need evidence — just repetition.

Kids don't question Santa Claus,

and they sure as hell don't question why Dad loses his mind at a stoplight.

And the older we get, the smarter hate gets.

It doesn't shout anymore — it influences.

It hides inside algorithms, pulpits, podcasts, and politicians.

It dresses up as "justice," "patriotism," or "common sense."

And before you know it, we're not arguing facts anymore —

we're arguing identities.

Because hate is easier to sell than nuance.

It's cheaper to produce than compassion.

And it's highly addictive.

But here's the good news:

If hate can be learned,

so can something better.

That's what this book is —

a manual for unlearning the reflex.

A field guide for choosing decency in a world that profits off your rage.

A dare to stay human — even when the world doesn't make it easy.

Hate is Visceral.

Kindness is resistance — the courage to transcend the ego's illusion of righteousness.

Once you hate, you have lost your humanity.

Prelude

Why We F*cking Hate People!

We hate the guy who cuts us off in traffic.

The woman who takes 47 items to the 10-items-or-less lane.

The coworker who says, "Just playing devil's advocate," right before saying something demonic.

The friend who says or does something off-color — maybe not even realizing it.

And don't even get me started on politics and international drama.

That's where hate stops being petty and starts getting *organized*.

But don't get too smug. Somewhere out there, you're probably the villain in someone else's perfectly justified story.

So where does all this hate actually come from?

It's not born overnight.

It's learned — drip by drip, meme by meme, argument by argument.

It hides inside pride, ego, insecurity, and the quiet satisfaction of feeling "right."

We absorb it from our parents, our peers, our newsfeeds — from the endless scroll that tells us who's to blame and why we're the heroes for blaming them.

Hate feels good at first. It gives us purpose, community, belonging.

JEFFREY ALAN

But like any addiction, it eventually turns on us.

Because hate doesn't just target "them." It corrodes *us*.

That's where this book starts — not with blame, but with honesty.

About how we got here.

And maybe, how we find our way back.

───────────

So let's start where hate shows up first — behind the wheel,
where everyone suddenly forgets they're human.

PART ONE

The Everyday Hate

The things that make us grind our teeth and roll our eyes —

the drivers, the Karens, the social media warriors,

the people who just don't "get it."

Part One explores the small annoyances that become big divides —

how bias, insecurity, and ego turn ordinary moments into battlegrounds.

Because before we can fix the world's hate,

we have to admit:

We practice it every day.

Chapter One

Raw Hate: Road Rage!

Primal hate on four wheels. Why tinted windows, anonymity, and ego create the perfect storm — and how humor can flip it

L et's start with something simple, and primal.

You, behind the wheel, losing your mind at a stranger you'll never meet again.

Road rage is humanity in its most condensed, caffeinated form.

It's the moment civilization unravels at 45 miles an hour because somebody in a Prius cut you off.

Your pulse spikes, your hand slams the horn, your brain lights up like a war room.

For five seconds, you're not a rational adult — you're a territorial animal defending two tons of steel and four feet of asphalt like it's sacred ground.

We've all been there.

And if you haven't, you either don't drive — or you don't drive in L.A.

Because Los Angeles isn't just a city. It's a psychological experiment in motion.

Every rush hour is a masterclass in suppressed rage and survival.

You can almost feel the air vibrating with stress, caffeine, and barely restrained middle fingers.

But here's the thing — road rage isn't random.

It's biology.

Humans evolved with a territorial reflex that once kept us alive in the wild.

Now that same instinct plays out in traffic.

When someone cuts you off, your brain doesn't register *lane change*.

It registers *attack*.

Your car becomes an extension of your personal space — your moving castle — and that Prius just stormed the drawbridge.

Then comes the flood: adrenaline, cortisol, a jolt of competition.

Your inner caveman grabs the wheel and says, "Not today, buddy."

That's how a merge lane becomes a battle for dominance.

Add environment to instinct, and you get L.A. — a city built to test patience like a lab rat in gridlock:

Congestion. Everyone's burning fuel and fuse.

Anonymity. Tinted windows turn faces into threats.

Status stress. Every Tesla and tow truck becomes a hierarchy test.

Heat. Science says irritation rises with temperature — and boy, does L.A. run hot.

So yes — the freeway is where empathy goes to die.

But it's also where understanding begins.

Because here's the twist: that guy cutting you off isn't *the enemy*.

He's a stressed-out human running late, just like you.

You can't see the kid crying in his back seat, or the sweat on his forehead, or the fact that he's just trying not to lose his job.

He stops being a person. He becomes "that asshole."

That's how hate starts — the moment we stop seeing faces and start seeing threats.

Tinted windows don't just block sunlight — they block empathy.

And that's the entire blueprint of this book.

We're all yelling at tinted windows — reacting to shadows instead of people.

The world's biggest fights often start with the smallest blind spots.

Bald Humor Hits Harder

I was cruising down La Brea Boulevard, doing that delicate L.A. dance between zen and insanity, when I hit a "construction zipper."

You know the one — two lanes merging into one, everyone pretending to be polite until they're not.

Then out of nowhere, this bald guy in a Prius guns it just to block me.

Instantly, my inner caveman woke up.

Blood boiling. Words loading.

But instead of rage, something surprising happened: I laughed.

Not the healthy kind — the unhinged kind.

Because right then, traffic karma staged a comedy sketch: the next red light trapped us side-by-side.

His window was down. Mine too.

Before I could think, I leaned out and said,

"Hey, handsome! Love your hair!"

He froze. Gripped the wheel.

And then, from the passenger seat, his wife's voice:

"WHAT DID HE SAY?"

That was it. Game over. My work there was done.

I laughed so hard I forgot to be angry.

Was it mean? Maybe.

Was it disarming? Absolutely.

That moment taught me something crucial:

You don't fight ego with ego.

You short-circuit it with humor.

Because rage feeds on resistance — but it starves in laughter.

A few months later, I found myself on the 405, watching a Dodge Challenger weave between cars like a demolition-derby dropout.

He cut me off so close I could see my reflection in his bumper.

Old me would've chased him.

But that day, the Bee Gees were blasting — *"Stayin' Alive"* on repeat — and all I thought was, *If you want to kill yourself, fine. But not me, not today.*

That was the moment it clicked.

I didn't rage. My pulse didn't spike. I didn't go into fight-or-flight mode.

Because I'd already built myself a new habit — my **Driving Playlist.**

Over a hundred songs that remind me who I am when I'm not pissed off.

Songs that melt the armor, soften the edges, and make me want to *wave* people in instead of running them off the road.

When someone cuts me off, I'll usually just wave them through.

And if I'm feeling extra zen — and their window's open — I might pull up, smile, and say,

"Hey champ — nice move. NASCAR would love you, but maybe ease up on the 405?"

Not a lecture. Just a little nudge wrapped in humor.

Because the goal isn't to win — it's to stay human.

HOW NOT TO F*CKING HATE PEOPLE: Road Rage

1. Road rage isn't about traffic — it's about control.

2. Prep your peace before you drive.

3. Humor disarms what ego inflames.

4. Music rewires the mood before anger can.

5. Control isn't about domination — it's about direction.

Chapter Two

Karens and Darrens: Driving the Mothership of Hate

Modern moral policing, viral outrage, and what coconut water can teach us about emotional intelligence

If road rage is primal hate in motion, Karen culture is what happens when that same instinct gets Wi-Fi and a rewards card.

Different vehicle, same engine.

Only now, instead of honking in traffic, people are honking online — in group chats, comment sections, and customer-service lines.

We used to complain to the manager.

Now we *become* the manager — of morality, politics, and everyone else's business.

Everyone's got a camera, a cause, and a craving to be right.

And here's the kicker:

We all have a little Karen or Darren living inside us.

That self-righteous voice that whispers, *Did they really just say that?* right before you open your mouth and lose your soul.

Karening is the modern form of territorial behavior.

You're not protecting your parking spot anymore — you're protecting your opinion.

And when that opinion gets challenged, your brain reacts exactly like it does behind the wheel:

Threat detected. Engage defense mode.

That's why a Facebook comment section looks like a freeway pile-up — only with more emojis and fewer survivors.

———

The Talk Show Effect

It's not just "Karens" in the wild, of course.

They come in many forms:

Mask Karen — still haunting grocery aisles from 2020, fighting over air.

Political Darren — who won't let you finish a sentence without reminding you who *really* ruined America.

Spiritual Karen — who weaponizes crystals.

Fitness Darren — who thinks your soul would be purer if you just tried intermittent fasting.

And the latest? The Ball-Grabbing Karen (not what you think, lol).

But the mother of them all — the Queen Karen of the Mothership — lives on daytime television.

You know the one: the show where five people sit around a table, talking over each other until you can't remember who's arguing or why.

It's like watching a family reunion hosted by caffeine and unresolved trauma.

And yet, it's the perfect microcosm of everything that's gone wrong.

Because they're not really debating.

They're *performing*.

They're fighting for applause, not understanding.

Each one has a side, a brand, a hashtag.

It's the same reason we feel exhausted after scrolling for ten minutes — everyone's yelling, but no one's listening.

And when we stop listening, hate grows in the silence.

Disarming the Mothership

Then something unexpected happened.

A content creator named **Damon Imani** decided to do what few could — face the Mothership itself.

He started making satirical videos, inserting himself right into clips of the show — not to scream back, but to *speak through the noise.*

No shouting. No theatrics.

Just calm, cutting truth delivered with humor and grace.

And people went crazy for it.

Because after years of watching everyone argue louder and meaner, calm suddenly felt like rebellion.

Imani didn't fight hate with hate — he held it accountable with wit.

He turned outrage into art.

He proved that humor isn't surrender — it's strategy.

It's proof that kindness doesn't mean silence.

It means control.

And when you keep your cool in a world that profits off chaos, you take the power back.

The Coconut Water Conversion

And that's exactly what happened at my store one afternoon.

A living, breathing Darren walked in — no yelling, no theatrics, just dripping with quiet entitlement.

It's a small health-and-fitness bodega I own in Hollywood — a real neighborhood place.

We know our customers by name.

We talk. We connect.

It's not Erewhon — it's friendlier, cheaper, and we actually mean it when we say hi.

This guy walks in, grabs our most popular coconut water — the one you can only get from us or Erewhon (for twice the price).

He slams it on the counter, eyes glued to his phone.

"Hey man," I say, "How's your day?"

Nothing.

Maybe he didn't hear me.

So I try again.

Still nothing.

No headphones. No hearing aids. Just pure, unfiltered disregard.

So I mimic his move — I pick up the coconut water and set it down behind the register with the same force, hoping *that* would get his attention.

Then I wait.

He finally looks up, realizes nothing's happening, and does the universal impatient hand gesture — *come on, let's go.*

So I mirror it. Perfectly.

"How's your day?" I ask again.

He looks me dead in the eyes. "Are you serious?"

"Very," I say. "How's your day?"

He mutters under his breath and storms out.

But twenty steps later, he's back — because he knows he can't get that coconut water anywhere else.

"Can I please have my drink?" he asks, now a little sheepish.

"Sure," I smile. "How's your day?"

He exhales — that long, deflated sigh of someone realizing this might not be the hill to die on.

"You're really doing this, aren't you?" he says.

"Yeah," I tell him. "We're a small neighborhood store. We take time to say hi and get to know our customers. There's no place for negative energy here. If you want something transactional, try a few doors down — but human being to human being... how's your day?"

"Fine," he says. "Are you happy now?"

"Yeah," I grin. "Now smile."

And he did — just a flicker, that half-grin people make when they've been humanized against their will.

He took his drink, left... and twenty steps later, turned back.

"You know what?" he said. "I'm really sorry. I was a jerk. I've just had a horrible day."

I nodded. "I get it. My dad's not doing too well right now. But I'm not taking it out on anyone. We all have stuff going on. When you meet kindness with negativity, you just make everything heavier. I'm trying to make it lighter — for both of us."

He paused. Nodded again.

No snark. No pretense. Just human.

Now? He's one of my best customers.

And half the time, he beats me to the question: "How's your day?"

That's the secret.

You don't tame a Karen (or Darren) by tolerating them.

You disarm them — by holding them accountable with grace.

Because when you speak truth calmly, they finally have to hear themselves.

And that's where the change begins.

HOW NOT TO F*CKING HATE PEOPLE: Karens & Darrens

1. The louder someone gets, the smaller they feel. Don't match their volume — master your own calm.

2. When you meet a Karen or a Darren, don't feed the fire — redirect the flame.

3. Stand your ground. Speak calm truth — not performative peace.

4. Let them know their behavior doesn't fly here — because you respect yourself.

5. You don't tame a Karen by exploding — you disarm them by holding the mirror steady.

6. Boundaries aren't aggression. They're clarity wrapped in self-respect.

7. Grace doesn't mean surrender. It means strength with composure.

8. The goal isn't to win the argument — it's to end the circus.

9. The world doesn't need fewer Karens. It needs more people who refuse to become one.

Kindness is Free.

INTERMISSION

Up Next: The Family Storm

You've survived the highways and the Karens.
You've learned to laugh at chaos, hold your ground with humor,
and maybe even see a little humanity hiding behind someone else's bad day.
Now the terrain changes — and the next chapter is a real doozie.
It's not about strangers who cut you off or people pushing hateful narratives;
it's about the ones you love, have loved, or who once loved you.
The people who helped build your hot buttons and revenge reflexes in the first place.
The ones who taught you their version of plurality —
love and hate in the same sentence.
So breathe.
Shake off the road dust.
Check your emotional mirrors and grab a drink.
We're leaving public traffic and heading home —
where kindness has to work without a speed limit.

Chapter Three

Friends and "Frenemies"

How to Stay Kind When They Mess Up — and When You Do Too

Most friendships don't end in betrayal.

They end in silence — after one person, maybe inadvertently, said or did the wrong thing, or was insensitive without realizing it.

We're comfortable with each other, and sometimes we make mistakes.

Sometimes those mistakes feel unforgivable… or so we think.

There's a good chance the person (or couple, group, or family) on the receiving end didn't know how to respond or how to say it hurt — so they never did.

They let it sit there like an unremovable stain on the friendship.

And slowly, that relationship dissolves — not with a fight, but with silence, less contact, colder dialogue, and missed meetings (some on purpose).

A cold shoulder. An arm's-length kind of distance.

Maybe hoping the other person will realize the error of their ways and come back with a mea culpa.

But it rarely happens — because the "offender" often doesn't even know what they did wrong.

And the person who was hurt doesn't have the tools — or the courage — to say so.

So it's easier to chalk it up to, *"They're just flawed. Irredeemable."*

And that becomes the new normal.

WTF? This person used to mean something to you.

Does a friendship not matter enough to you that it's easier to take the easy way out than do a little work to save — and maybe even strengthen — it?

We expect negative vibes from strangers who don't know us.

Not from friends.

But when it comes from someone who knows your favorite song, your middle name, or your worst day — that's when it cuts differently.

Especially when you never saw it coming.

Friendships don't implode because someone "forgets kindness."

They implode because someone says the wrong thing, doesn't show up, flakes on a promise, makes a bad joke, crosses a boundary, or just fails to read the room.

That's messing up.

And it happens to all of us.

We're all human.

Say that out loud: **WE. ARE. ALL. HUMAN.**

The real test of a friendship isn't whether you avoid those moments — it's how you handle them when they happen.

Do you double down?

Tell everyone what a terrible person they are?

Do you disappear?

Or do you take a breath, own it, and repair it before it calcifies into resentment?

Do you care enough to try?

Because every unspoken hurt becomes a quiet goodbye waiting to happen.

The Comfort Trap

Truth is, the closer we get to someone — the longer we know them — the more careless we can become.

Not because we stop caring, but because comfort tricks us into thinking connection is indestructible.

We speak without filters, joke without caution, and forget that even people who love us have limits, expectations, and personal codes of conduct.

Break one of those, and that's where the first crack forms.

That's the trap: comfort creates blind spots.

You think, *They know me, they'll get it.*

But what they actually get is hurt — and confusion.

You just flipped their definition of "appropriate" upside down.

They're wondering, *How could you say that? How do you not know better?*

Most of the time, insensitivity isn't intentional.

It doesn't come from cruelty or broken character — it comes from a bad assumption.

We assume that whatever we say or do — even if it's flippant — will be understood, that our tone will be forgiven, our joke will land, our advice will help.

But kindness without awareness can cut deep when we're not careful, or when we're tone-deaf to the moment.

We've all done it.

We're not perfect.

But we care — even if sometimes that care comes out wrong.

Gossip

Gossip is the soft cough in the crowded room — the subtle, polite start of an infection.

It sounds harmless: *"just saying," "just concerned," "just being honest."*

But every whisper is a contaminated exhale — one person's bitterness becoming someone else's assumption.

It spreads quietly, changing how we see each other, how we trust, how we love.

Hate doesn't always shout; sometimes it just gossips.

Gossip is the breath that carries the virus of hate.

Stop and recognize what's really happening. The intent.

Because, by the time you realize what it's done, it's already changed how you see people.

That's how hate spreads — disguised as conversation.

When They're the One Who Messed Up

Someone you care about said something tone-deaf.

Did something selfish. Acted rude or said something insensitive.

Missed a moment that mattered to you.

Maybe they were careless. Maybe they were clueless.

Said the wrong thing in public. Missed the moment that mattered most.

In the end — maybe they were just human.

But now you're sitting with that sting — the mix of disappointment, anger, and sadness that comes from realizing someone who knows you... somehow didn't *see* you.

It's easy to write them off.

Easier to get cold than to get clear.

Easier to tell yourself you've outgrown them than to risk an awkward conversation.

After all, who needs a friend who acts like that?

You don't give them the grace you'd want for yourself.

You thought they were perfect — that they thought exactly like you.

Then you realized... they're not.

But here's the thing: they *are* (or were) your friend.

Don't they deserve the same grace you'd hope for in return?

Not every wound is a dealbreaker.

Some are just unspoken lessons waiting to be aired out and understood. That's growth.

Most friendships don't die from betrayal.

They die from neglect. From silence.

From the story we start telling ourselves when the other person doesn't explain.

We fill in the blanks with judgment:

"They should've known better."

"They obviously don't care."

"They're showing their true colors."

Sometimes we're right.   But sometimes... we're just hurt.

So what do you do when the person who hurt you doesn't even realize they did?

You start with curiosity, not accusation.

You communicate. Remember when talking was easy?

Try:

> *"Hey, can we talk about something that's been bugging me? I really care about you and our friendship, but when you [insert specific moment], it landed differently than I think you meant."*

or

> *"I know you probably didn't mean it this way, but that comment really stung."*

That's not weakness. That's strength.

You're giving them a chance to rise — or reveal who they really are.

If they are a real friend, they'll meet you there.

They'll listen, own it, and work to repair it.

If they're not — their reaction will tell you everything you need to know.

Either way, you win.

Because you showed up with integrity and authenticity.

Kindness doesn't mean tolerating bad behavior.

It means addressing it with backbone and grace.

It's saying, *"I value this friendship enough to be honest — and I respect myself enough to draw a line if I need to."*

And yes, sometimes the healthiest thing you can do is step back.

Not out of hate, but out of self-respect.

Forgiveness doesn't always mean reconnection.

It means freeing yourself from the bitterness that keeps you stuck in their mistake.

You can wish someone well and still walk away.

You can appreciate the best parts of them and still know you can't peacefully have them in your life again.

That's acceptance. **You can let go without turning them into a villain.**

That's not weakness — that's evolution.

And if they ever come back open, humble, and ready to repair what they broke — meet them halfway.

You'll know by then whether the bridge is still worth crossing.

Because real friendship isn't about never hurting each other.

It's about learning how to heal without turning love into leverage.

When You're the One Who Messed Up

I know, you're probably saying to yourself, *Who, me?*

Yes, you. We've all been that person.

The one who said the wrong thing. Did the wrong thing.

Missed the signal. Missed the opportunity.

Laughed when we shouldn't have. Spoke when we shouldn't have.

Said the wrong thing when we did. Didn't read the room. Seemed oblivious or self-centered.

Offered advice when we were supposed to just listen.

Sometimes it's small — a tone, a text, a careless word.

Sometimes it's big — a broken confidence, a selfish choice, or a moment of pure emotional clumsiness.

But here's the bigger truth:

Messing up doesn't make you a bad person.

Not being able to receive constructive feedback — or own it — does.

This doesn't mean you can't discuss it like an adult, or even defend what you said or did if you truly believe you weren't in the wrong.

But you have to at least let the other person speak their heart.

More often than not, if you truly listen, you'll realize where the car derailed — and you can apologize, get back on track and keep the relationship moving forward.

If you want to.

The most powerful sentence in any friendship isn't *"I'm right."*

It's *"You're right — and I'm sorry."*

But only if you mean it.

And only if you're truly committed to the friendship.

And sometimes you'll be surprised — after you've both been able to speak your truth, you might hear those same words coming back to you.

Because they love you too.

And they're just as committed to saving what you built before things went sideways.

Those five words can rebuild years.

They say: *I see you. I value this. You matter more than my ego.*

But most people never say them.

Because admitting fault feels like losing power — when in reality, it's what restores it.

And yes, it's hard.

You have to let go of your ego, even if only for two seconds.

You have to feel it — really feel it — and mean it.

Here's the paradox of kindness:

You can't fix what you won't face.

Let your ego go, especially when it comes to the most meaningful relationships in your life.

Because sometimes, the most loving thing you can do is sit in your own discomfort long enough to understand how it felt on their end.

So how do you do that?

You stop defending your *intent* and start acknowledging their *impact*.

Because here's the thing:

You don't get to decide what hurt someone.

You only get to decide whether you care enough to make it right.

Maybe you didn't mean to be dismissive.

Maybe your joke was just a joke.

Maybe your silence wasn't meant as rejection.

But if someone you care about tells you it hurt — it did.

Your job isn't to debate that; it's to understand it.

That's the difference between a mature friendship and a fragile one.

Fragile friendships demand perfection.

Mature ones allow repair.

Owning it doesn't mean groveling.

It means humility.

It means saying, *"I messed up. You didn't deserve that. Help me understand how to do better."* **And mean it.**

And then — this is the hard part — you listen.

Without explaining.

Without turning it back around.

Without saying, *"Well, you did this too."*

Just listen.

Because when you give someone space to be heard, you give the friendship a chance to breathe again.

And if they're not ready to talk yet?

Respect the space.

Apologies aren't transactions — they're offerings.

You put them on the table and walk away knowing you meant it.

If they value the friendship as much as you do, they'll think about it — and appreciate you for being open to their hurt, for *seeing them.*

Because that's what real friendship — real relationship — is about: seeing each other and accepting each other for who we are.

Unless your worldviews have completely diverged, your friendship will survive.

That's the kind of ownership that keeps love alive long after pride should've killed it.

Kindness is Free.

HOW NOT TO F*CKING HATE PEOPLE: Friends and Frenemies

1. Most people don't mean to wound you. You're their friend, not their target.
   Your ego will try to convince you otherwise. Don't let it.

2. Communicate with kindness and grace.
   Ask, don't accuse. Curiosity builds bridges that blame can't cross.

3. Speak up.
   Don't let silence unfairly rewrite the story.

4. Gossip. Don't!

5. Choose repair over being right.
   Pride feels powerful for a minute; honest connection built on accountability lasts a lifetime.

6. Own it.
   Appreciate the feedback.

7. "I'm sorry" isn't weakness — it's damage control with dignity.
   Say it — calmly.

8. Kind truth beats quiet bitterness every time.

9. Listen like you actually want to keep them.
   Don't reload while they're still talking.

10. Forgive to free yourself.
    You can't move forward while replaying the last scene.

11. And if it's over, let it end clean.
    No gossip. No scorekeeping. Gratitude, then goodbye.

12. Because kindness doesn't mean swallowing your pain —
    it means handling it without losing your humanity.

Chapter Four

The Everyday Fights

How to Stay Kind When People Suck (Just a Little...or a lot!)

Before we get to the global hate, the media outrage, and the moral chaos that make headlines,

let's talk about the smaller fires — the everyday ones that quietly burn inside us.

Most hate doesn't start on a battlefield.

It starts in a text left unanswered.

A rude comment at a coffee shop.

A slowpoke driver pinning the needle at the speed limit while the lane next to you flies by.

These aren't wars. They're *micro-collisions* — the little hits that, left unchecked, turn good people bitter.

So this chapter isn't philosophy. It's practice.

For each of these, you'll see three things:

On the following pages, you'll find everyday situations that make even the calmest person want to scream, quit humanity, or pull their hair out.

You've lived these moments — in traffic, in line, online, at work.

Each one is universal, the kind of thing people tell me about every single day at the store.

Here's how it works

What triggers you. What it does to you. And how to respond without losing your humanity.

Because real kindness doesn't live in theories or hashtags.

It lives in the everyday fights — when people suck just a little... or a lot

My hope is that after reading these, you'll start to see them a little differently — not as proof that people are terrible, but as opportunities to practice something better.

It's not every frustration you'll ever face, but it's a start.

Because learning to handle the small stuff with kindness and grace is how we get strong enough to face the big stuff.

———————

Ghosting

What triggers you:

You match. You message. You swap pics — maybe even albums.

The vibe's good. The banter's easy. The build-up is hot.

You're excited, and you assume they are too.

They say all the right things — the flirty texts, the late-night *"you up?"* energy — and for a minute, it feels like you found something real, or at least someone fun to take you away from the digital chaos.

And then — if you're lucky — you meet.

Things go great. Neither of you wants the night to end.

When it does, you giddily exchange numbers and promise to see each other again.

She says she'll text when she gets home.

But the text never arrives.

You've been through this before, but this time felt different.

You get worried. You text: *Everything okay? You home?*

No reply.

Message unread.

Then, the next day — you realize she's blocked you.

No explanation. No *"sorry, not feeling it."*

Just silence that starts to feel personal.

What it does to you:

At first, you brush it off. *I hope she's okay.*

Then the block hits. That's when it stings.

You replay every text, every photo, every pause.

You start thinking: *Was I too much? Too forward? Not hot enough? Not cool enough?*

It's wild how fast one person's silence can turn your confidence into a crime scene.

You feel disposable — like a story someone half-started and got bored of writing.

And this is only the fifth time it's happened.

Rest assured — it's not you.

It's what our culture has become: people are disposable until they don't want to be.

Blame it on gaming culture.

Most people on dating and hookup apps grew up in a world that rewards exploration, conquest... and reset.

There's no moral weight to leaving a game mid-round.

Encounters become rounds instead of relationships.

And when the round's over, the instinct is to exit. Simple as that.

How to respond without losing your humanity:

First, stop taking their disappearance as a reflection of your worth.

It's not. This is a *game* to them.

Ghosting isn't about you — it's about them not having the emotional maturity to break out of that mindset, see you as a person, and act like an adult.

So don't chase them.

Don't double-text. Don't send the *"?"* or the *"Did I do something wrong?"*

You didn't.

Delete the thread.

Block if you have to.

And thank the universe for showing you who they are — before you got invested.

You don't want to be with someone who plays games — literally — with your heart.

Because the truth is, ghosting is emotional laziness.

And you're not here for that.

Lesson:

The right person — whether they want a date, a weekend, or something real — won't make you guess.

Kindness here means not matching their cowardice.

Wish them well (silently). Then move on like a damn adult — because they didn't.

The Slowpoke Driver

What triggers you:

You're finally on time for once — coffee in hand, playlist on point — when your lane slows to a crawl.

Cars fly past you in the next lane, but no one's letting you in.

You inch forward, waiting for your moment, and then you see it:

a little Prius pinning the needle at 30 in a 45.

And you're stuck.

You've lost control.

You can't change lanes or escape.

Meanwhile, other cars stream past, and your brain starts narrating:

They're getting ahead. I'm stuck.

It's primitive status anxiety dressed up as traffic.

What it does to you:

Your nervous system reads it as danger, not inconvenience.

Cortisol spikes. Adrenaline joins the party.

Fight or flight — with nowhere to go.

The tension builds: first in your stomach, then your chest, then your jaw.

You're gripping the wheel like it owes you money.

The light ahead turns red.

No one in the next lane shows mercy.

"Oh my God, I'm gonna be late again because of this idiot."

You start writing their backstory:

They're clueless. They're smug. They're the reason society's falling apart.

And then — finally — a miracle.

One kind soul catches your eye and waves you in.

You slip into the next lane. You breathe — humanity, restored.

Your cortisol drops. You relax. You move on.

How to respond without losing your humanity:

Name the real threat.

Silently say: *This isn't danger; it's delay.*

Take a deep breath.

If you're late, the world won't end.

Reset expectations.

Estimate how late you'll be.

Make a quick call or send a text:

> *"Hey, traffic's a little slow — might be five minutes behind."*

Pressure released. Problem solved.

Choose to relax.

Take another breath.

Smile. The crisis is over.

Maybe the universe has a different plan for you.

Maybe this delay *is* the plan.

It's not always about you.

Re-story the moment.

Try humor or compassion:

Maybe they just got bad news. Maybe this is my reminder to chill.

It's not moral weakness — it's emotional regulation.

Lesson:

You can't control the road.

But you can control your ride.

Every slow driver is a crash course in patience — literally

———————

The Line Cutter

What triggers you:

You've been waiting. Patiently.

Coffee line, airport boarding, TSA checkpoint — doesn't matter. You've done the time.

And then *they* appear.

The line cutter.

Phone in hand, pretending to be oblivious while sliding right in front of you like it's their birthright.

They avoid eye contact, fidget, maybe fake a phone call.

You feel that pulse of disbelief rise — *Are you kidding me?*

You look back, hoping someone else will say something.

They don't.

So now it's on you — judge, jury, and witness protection.

What it does to you:

That small act lights up your brain like a five-alarm fire.

It's not about the latte or the minutes you'll lose — it's about *justice*.

It's the principle.

Someone just broke the unspoken social contract, and you've been elected as the only one who noticed.

Your heartbeat quickens.

Your body leans forward.

It's not just irritation — it's a primal demand for fairness.

Because deep down, the mind equates cutting the line with cutting respect.

And that triggers everything in you that hates being unseen.

How to respond without losing your humanity:

First, breathe. Seriously.

This isn't the revolution. It's a coffee shop.

Now, assess the risk.

If they look like they could handle correction, use calm confidence:

"Hey, the line actually starts back there."

Say it clearly. No sarcasm, no venom — just authority wrapped in civility.

If they ignore you? Your choice:

Let it go and reclaim your peace. (Your coffee will still taste the same.)

Or, for sport, hit them with humor:

"Unless you've got a FastPass for lattes, line's back there."

Either way, you win — because you stayed in control.

If it escalates — walk away.

You don't need to go to war over a latte.

The goal isn't to *win* the moment. It's to *win* your peace of mind.

Lesson:

You can't fix entitlement with anger.

But you can model calm authority — and walk out with caffeine and class.

———————

The Gym Rat

What triggers you:

You're mid-set, in your zone, when it happens:

The Grunter. The Slamm-er. The Protein-Prophet.

He's shirtless, loud, and making the gym sound like a medieval forge.

He's using two benches — one for his towel and water bottle, one for his ego.

What it does to you:

You came to lift your mood, not your cortisol.

But here he is — your personal test in restraint.

Every slam of the weights jolts your focus.

You feel it in your temples, your chest, your urge to narrate:

We get it, bro. You have triceps and trauma.

You fantasize about dropping a dumbbell near his foot — not to hurt, just to remind.

But you don't.

Because you're not trying to end up in a viral gym video titled *"Rage Guy vs. Chad."*

How to respond without losing your humanity:

Option one: humor.

Walk by and say, "Damn, man — the floor's already impressed."

Option two: calm assertion.

"Hey, mind if I work in between sets?"

Confidence, not confrontation.

Then reclaim your zone.

Put in your earbuds.

Refocus on why you came.

His noise can't touch your peace when you're in the zone (with noise cancellation)

Lesson:

You don't have to match volume to prove strength.

Kindness here is composure — because calm is contagious,

and nothing rattles a show-off like someone who doesn't need an audience.

Preauthorization Hell

What triggers you:

You're sick, stressed, or scared — or worse, trying to take care of someone who is.

Your doctor orders a test, a scan, or a medication you've never taken before.

Time is of the essence. This is your health.

You assume it's covered. You call the pharmacy to check on the prescription.

"I'm sorry, sir — we're unable to proceed until your insurance provider issues preauthorization."

So you call your insurance company.

Forty-five minutes later, you're connected — to a rep halfway around the world.

They're kind. Scripted.

And completely powerless.

They ask you to "verify" everything: address, date of birth, ID number — maybe even your childhood pet if it's on file.

You explain the situation, calmly at first.

They don't understand the terminology, the urgency.

Then they tell you it appears your doctor sent the order in at the end of the day.

It's Friday — and no one can get to it until Monday.

There's nothing they can do.

What it does to you:

It spikes your cortisol through the stratosphere.

You don't need more health issues — so calm down.

But it's too late; the fuse is lit.

Suddenly, your hatred for health insurance companies feels *earned*.

You feel invisible in the system that's supposed to protect you.

You realize you're not a person anymore — you're a policy number.

So you take it out on the rep, fantasizing that somehow your anger will echo through the company and fix everything.

You start talking louder — not because you're rude, but because helplessness has nowhere else to go.

You know this person isn't the villain, but they're part of the machine.

Maybe, you think, they'll take your plight to the top.

They won't — but rage still wants a target. And a result.

By the time you hang up, you feel guilty — for losing it, for caring so much, for still not having an answer.

You realize the system isn't broken by accident.

It's designed to wear you down until you stop asking.

How to respond without losing your humanity:

Before the next call on Monday, take a long, deep breath.

Name what's really happening:

This isn't one person's fault — it's a flawed system held together by duct tape and red tape.

You're not alone in it. Trust me — we're *all* living this nightmare.

So don't scream. It won't help.

But kindness might.

Start your call right.

Say hello. Listen to the rep's name.

Say it back when you ask how *their* day is going.

People don't do that anymore.

They'll notice — and they'll appreciate it.

You'll stand out from the 99 other people who will yell at them today.

That rep will *want* to help you.

Empathy cuts through automation faster than anger ever will.

Then document everything — starting with their name.

That signals to them that there's a potential positive review in their future if they can actually solve your problem.

Now you've turned them into an ally.

Stay calm, firm, and relentlessly polite.

You'll hear the shift — that moment when they stop reading the script and start *really* helping.

Because someone finally treated them like a person, too.

Lesson:

Kindness here isn't compliance — it's control.

Don't let a broken system make you break your character.

Stay calm. Stay clear. Stay kind.

Because the person on the other end probably hates this process as much as you do.

I saw the perfect slogan on a hat once that fits this perfectly:

Live more. Worry less.

———————

Feeling Invisible

What triggers you:

You walk into a room, event, or group chat — and you almost feel like you don't belong.

The conversations are already flowing, the laughter already formed.

You hover for a second, waiting for someone to make eye contact — but they don't.

You smile. You nod. Nothing.

It's that uneasy feeling — that quiet, sinking realization that you've entered a space that's already decided who matters here.

What it does to you:

It's subtle, but it hits hard.

That mix of embarrassment, irritation, and self-doubt bubbles up.

You tell yourself you don't care — but you do.

Your body tenses, your voice retreats, and your brain starts whispering lies: *You're not interesting enough. You're not one of them. You don't fit.*

So you armor up.

You pretend you're above it. You scroll your phone. You leave early.

But later — when it's quiet — it lingers.

Because exclusion doesn't just bruise your ego; it bruises your humanity.

How to respond without losing your humanity:

Pause the story your brain is writing.

Most people don't exclude out of malice — they do it out of fear, habit, or comfort.

Look around the room.

There's usually someone else who feels just as out of place.
Walk up, introduce yourself.

And if no one stands out, find that one person who's drifted slightly from the group — the one checking their phone or their drink — and say hello.

There's a good chance they'll pull you in and start introducing you around.

Because cliques aren't always cruelty — sometimes they're just comfort zones.

And most people in them would still love to meet someone new…

if you give them the chance.

Lesson:

Kindness here isn't waiting to be seen — it's daring to be the first one to say hello.

And just when you think you've mastered kindness… life sends you the bill.

———————

I'll Venmo You

What triggers you:

Dinner's been great — laughter, drinks, the kind of conversation that makes you forget to check your phone.

The check lands.

They're quick — as they always are — with the casual line:

"Hey, want to just pay it? I'll Venmo or Apple Pay you."

You nod. Sure. Easy.

Why you keep doing this, you don't know.

You watch them pull out their phone, tap the screen… and then get distracted by something on Instagram.

So the *ding* never comes.

Hours pass. You casually mention it.

"Don't worry, I'll pay you!"

They say it with that annoyed tone — like *you're* the one being unreasonable for reminding them about something *they* offered to do after *you* did them a favor.

Nothing.

Days pass. A week. Still nothing.

Finally, you nudge:

"Hey, I never got your Venmo."

Cue the sigh, the deflection, the guilt trip:

"Wow, okay. I said I'd send it. You're so uptight. Here. Happy?"

And suddenly, you feel like shit.

You're not the nice one anymore — you're the problem for expecting follow-through.

What it does to you:

It's not about the money — it's about the shift.

You feel like they're toying with you. Like it's some kind of sick game.

And the worst part? This isn't the first time.

It's become a pattern — and now it's your job to break it.

They've turned your kindness into a convenience.

Maybe they even enjoy watching you squirm — what a great friend.

But then you start replaying the night, wondering if you're overreacting… again.

Deep down, though, you know it wasn't an accident.

It's a power move — a quiet way of saying, *my word doesn't have to mean much, but you'll still say yes next time.*

Because you're kind. Because you still believe people can do better.

But they won't — not until you stop giving them the chance to treat you like a tab they never plan to close.

How to respond without losing your humanity:

If you want to keep this friend, next time play offense.

Send the Venmo or Apple Pay request *before* you pay the bill — no emoji, no apology, just clarity.

If they don't send it, that's your answer.

Don't pay the whole bill.

Flag the waiter. Ask for separate checks.

No sarcasm. No anger. Just a boundary.

People who respect you will never make you chase fairness.

The rest — they can keep their IOUs.

Lesson:

Kindness isn't about covering for other people's character flaws.

It's about knowing when grace becomes permission.

Because friendship without integrity and reciprocity isn't really friendship at all — is it?

Kindness is Free.

Chapter Five

Cancelling Cancel Culture

When the World Tries to Cancel You — and You Refuse to Play Along

Dogma isn't just religious — it's any inherited script that tells us who deserves love, who deserves forgiveness, and who doesn't.

It's the quiet architecture of judgment, built long before we even realize we're living by its rules.

It tells us how to live, love, and behave — and sometimes, what to hate.

We inherit it from parents, pastors, teachers, and politicians.

We internalize it as "the right path," and then pass it down like a family heirloom.

And while it's meant to protect us, it often does the opposite — it boxes us in.

But here's the thing: when we follow something blindly, it's not faith anymore. It's programming.

And when programming meets pain, the outcome is predictable — cancellation.

That's where cancel culture was really born — not online, but around dinner tables, in family arguments, and inside the quiet shame of people who don't fit the mold.

I've lived that.

And I've learned that the only way to cancel that kind of cancel culture isn't through anger — it's through kindness.

What follows are three stories — three moments where love, faith, and identity collided — and how compassion cracked them open.

Act One — When Love Changes Shape

The Fallout

When I came out, my marriage ended.

And the fallout wasn't just heartbreak — it was chaos.

My ex-wife was young, hurt, and blindsided. She couldn't grasp the idea of a loving separation. To her, my truth felt like betrayal.

Her mother — protective and wounded in her own right — stood by her side, trying to make sense of something that felt like loss and confusion all at once. And in their pain, I became the villain in a story none of us had written intentionally.

It felt like every move I made was misinterpreted, every attempt to make peace somehow proof that I didn't care. Frozen accounts, tense phone calls, lawyers on speed dial.

Everything that once bound us — love, children, shared dreams — became evidence in an emotional courtroom neither of us wanted to be in.

Sound familiar?

That's cancel culture up close.

Not the social-media kind — the *family* kind, where someone decides your truth invalidates theirs, so the only way to feel safe again is to erase you.

The Realization

Even then, I never saw coming out as destruction.

I saw it as love.

For her — because she deserved a husband who could love her fully and authentically.

For me — because after thirty-nine years, I finally stopped lying about who I was.

For God — because the real sin wasn't *how* I was made; it was denying it.

God doesn't make mistakes.

People do.

The fallout hurt, but when the smoke cleared, what remained was gratitude — for the years we had, the family we built, and the lessons we both had to learn the hard way.

I wouldn't wish that pain on anyone, but I wouldn't erase it either. It forced me to rebuild from the ground up.

It brought me back to L.A., back to my parents, back to myself.

If I hadn't walked through that fire, you wouldn't be holding this book.

And if she or her family ever read these words, I hope they don't feel judged — only seen.

We were all just trying to survive something bigger than us.

And sometimes, surviving is its own act of grace.

Act Two — The Father Test

The Confrontation

My father was a proud man — disciplined, traditional, and rooted in faith.

He wasn't cruel, but warmth wasn't his language.

His approval always felt like something to *earn*.

One evening, we were sitting at the dinner table — me, my parents, and a close friend beside me. It had been a surprisingly easy night, full of laughter and calm.

Then my friend's pinky brushed mine as I reached for my soup spoon. My dad caught it and said flatly:

"You know, Jeff, I may not approve of your chosen lifestyle, but I guess I have no choice but to deal with it. I just don't accept it."

The warmth evaporated.

My friend froze.

My heart pounded.

I could've snapped or stormed out.

But this time, I chose kindness — not silence, *kindness with backbone.*

The Realization

His language was faith, so I spoke in it.

I told him how long it had taken me to find peace — decades of wrestling with myself, my faith, and the God we both believed in.

How I'd searched scripture for answers, diving into the original Hebrew, until I found the truth that changed everything:

the verse weaponized against men like me wasn't about love — it was about *violence*.

The sin wasn't being gay.

It was using love as domination or control.

That distinction shattered the chains I'd carried for years.

So I asked him:

"Dad, you believe God doesn't make mistakes, right?"

"Of course."

"Then if you have a problem with me — take it up with Him. Because you, Mom, and God made me. And I'm no mistake."

Then I said, calmly,

"I'm going to live the life I was created to live. No apologies. Because this isn't sin. It's love. It's light. And it's exactly how God made me."

Silence.

Then — a smile.

From him. From my mom.

The battle ended, never to be fought again.

For the first time, I felt peace.

Act Three — When Empathy Stops at the Border

The Breakdown

My friend Mateo came into my store one Monday looking wrecked.

He's one of those people who usually lights up a room — the kind of guy who laughs with his whole chest and somehow makes everyone else do the same.

But that day, the light was gone.

He told me it had been a brutal weekend.

His best friend's father and brother had been picked up in an ICE raid.

His uncle — who'd lived here for thirty years — was still waiting for his green card.

And even though Mateo was born here, his parents were terrified every time they left the house.

They'd worked for decades — two jobs each, saving every dollar — and finally earned their green cards just three years ago.

They didn't come here legally.

They came here *desperately*.

They built a life out of fear, sweat, and hope that someday they'd be seen as equal.

The Blind Spot

Then he told me what broke him.

He'd opened up about it to his girlfriend — the woman he thought he'd marry.

He told her about the raid, the fear, the exhaustion, the gratitude.

And she said, flatly:

"If people want to come here, they should just do it legally."

He said it felt like being punched in the chest.

He tried to explain.

That "legal" wasn't an option for his parents when they came.

That they'd spent half their lives earning the right she got just by being born on the right side of a line.

But she didn't want to understand. She wanted to feel *right*.

The irony?

She was from Canada — here on a visa that had long expired.

But she didn't see herself as "illegal."

She saw herself as *different*.

Because privilege has a way of disguising itself as innocence.

He kept trying — gently, patiently — to help her see the complexity.

But the more human he became, the colder she got.

The Cancellation

By Sunday, it was over.

No fight. Just silence.

And in that silence, he realized it wasn't just a breakup.

It was a cancellation — quiet but complete.

She wasn't rejecting a person; she was erasing a story.

His story.

The story of a family who crossed borders for survival, who worked thirty years to earn belonging.

The story of millions who love a country that doesn't always love them back.

She wasn't curious.

She was comfortable.

And comfort doesn't ask questions — it cancels them.

He saw who she truly was.

And maybe, for the first time, she saw who he truly was too — someone whose worth didn't need her approval to exist.

That's the kind of cancel culture no one talks about.

The kind that hides behind politics and "principles."

The kind that turns empathy into a border.

_____

Act Four — The Dinner That Changed Everything

The Invitation

At one point, I was traveling regularly to Salt Lake City for work.

That's where I met him — a kind, impossibly handsome Mormon guy named Jakob.

We started seeing each other quietly — nothing dramatic, just connection in the middle of desert air.

One night, when I said I wished we lived closer, he sighed:

"You know, Jeff, we can never really be serious. My parents expect me to marry a woman. I'm just trying to live my life until then."

It wasn't cruelty. It was resignation.

He'd been told since birth that love had to look a certain way — and defying that meant losing everything.

A week later, he asked me to join his family's *Family Home Evening* — prayer, hymns, dinner.

He wanted them to see I wasn't a threat. Just real.

So I went.

The Conversation

Dinner was beautiful — warm, reverent, full of laughter.

But curiosity buzzed beneath the politeness.

After dinner, Jakob asked if we could speak privately. His parents agreed.

He introduced me gently, like a gift.

Then asked if I'd share my story.

So I did — about my marriage, my faith, and how long it took to make peace with who I am.

I told them obedience without authenticity destroys everyone it touches.

Their son wasn't broken. He was brave. He was whole.

And I tied it all back to the commandment every faith forgets:

Love thy neighbor as thyself.

When I explained how scripture had been mistranslated and weaponized, both their eyes filled — not with shame, but understanding.

The Shift

By the end of the night, something softened.

They didn't wave rainbow flags — but the pressure stopped. The fear melted.

As I left, his mother hugged me and whispered,

"Thank you."

Driving back to my hotel, I realized something that's never left me:

Kindness isn't about convincing anyone.

It's about *disarming fear with truth.*

That dinner wasn't about conversion — it was about connection.

And yes — the pie was absolutely delicious.

> ### HOW NOT TO F*CKING HATE PEOPLE: Cancelling Cancel Culture
>
> 1. Don't confuse being *right* with being *good*.
> 2. When love changes shape, let it — without rewriting the other person as the villain.
> 3. Faith without empathy is just fear in scripture's clothing.
> 4. Speak truth in the language they understand — not to win, but to be heard.
> 5. When someone's blind spot hurts you, remember: ignorance isn't always malice — sometimes it's comfort refusing to grow.
> 6. Defend your boundaries without erasing someone else's story.
> 7. Don't mistake silence for weakness — some peace is earned through restraint.
> 8. Kindness doesn't mean compliance; it means refusing to surrender your humanity.
> 9. Curiosity is rebellion in a world addicted to certainty.
> 10. *When all else fails, love louder than their fear.*

Kindness is Free.

PART TWO

A GLOBAL PANDEMIC

When hate goes viral, it stops being personal — it becomes political, cultural, global.

Part Two explores how misinformation, outrage, and tribal loyalty shape the stories we tell and the sides we take.

Because the moment we stop asking *why* —

we start mistaking emotion for truth.

Whose Truth Is It Anyway?

There was a time when truth was something we searched for.
Now it's something that finds us — or rather, *chooses* us.
What we once called "history" is now rewritten in real time,
streamed through algorithms designed to confirm what we already believe.
We don't chase answers anymore;
we chase affirmation.
And somehow, over time,
the past has begun to disappear — not erased in one moment,
but quietly buried under updates and outrage.
They say those who forget the past are doomed to repeat it.
But what happens when entire generations never even knew it existed?
You see, no matter which side we stand on,
we're all staring through a different lens —
one crafted by what we click,
who we follow,
and what we fear.
Show two people the same image —
one sees oppression, the other sees defense.
Play the same clip —
one cries injustice, the other cheers victory.
Both feel certain. Both feel righteous.
Maybe the real threat isn't fake news —
maybe it's that we've forgotten how to tell the difference.
Because when every truth comes prepackaged with a villain and a hero,
the only thing left to question is ourselves.
So maybe the question isn't *"Who's lying?"*
Maybe it's something harder.
Maybe it's —
Whose truth is it anyway?

Chapter Seven

When Worldviews Collide

Some knots take more than one pair of hands to untie.

The world isn't breaking — it's fraying. Every argument, every headline, every "hot take" pulls another thread loose. And the louder we yell, the faster it unravels.

Right versus Left.

Good versus Evil.

Truth versus "Alternative Facts."

We've turned human existence into a never-ending courtroom drama — where everyone's a prosecutor, no one's a listener, and the jury's just the comment section.

What one side calls justice, the other calls hypocrisy.

What one side calls liberation, the other calls chaos.

We're all shouting into the void, desperate to be right instead of real.

And that's how hate hides — inside our righteousness.

It's not that people stopped caring. It's that caring became competitive.

We don't try to understand each other anymore; we try to win at empathy.

We call it "raising awareness," but most days it's just raising cortisol.

We've mistaken activism for algorithms.

Compassion for clicks.

Opinions for oxygen.

We've built our own prisons — walls made of confirmation bias and dopamine hits.

Every scroll tightens the knot.

And here's the worst part:

We've forgotten that truth doesn't need sides — it needs space.

So before we pick another fight, repost another sermon, or light another bridge, stop and ask yourself these four questions:

1. Can I still see someone as deserving of grace when their truth challenges mine?

2. Can I hold my own identity while respecting someone who can't reflect it back to me?

3. Can I face a truth that dismantles what I've always believed — and still stay open to it?

4. Can love exist when acceptance isn't absolute — when I'm "tolerated" but not respected?

Now flip them — because those same questions work both ways.

- *Can they see you with grace when your truth shakes theirs?*

- *Can they hold their identity without needing yours as a mirror?*

- *Can they face a truth that shatters their certainty — and be honest enough to evolve?*

- *Can they truly love you if they can't see all of you?*

That last one stings, doesn't it?

Because that's where most of us get stuck — we want unconditional acceptance from people who've never had to question their own conditions.

And the third one — about honesty and growth — might be the hardest of all.

We're starting to see what happens when people realize they were wrong.

When influencers backpedal, when politicians reframe, when ordinary people quietly evolve — those are the rare moments of real courage.

It takes a big person to admit they've outgrown their own certainty.

The question is:

Are you big enough?

Are they?

Those reversed questions are where clarity — and peace — begin.

Because kindness isn't just about how you treat others.

It's about recognizing when someone can't meet you there — and choosing to step back with grace instead of hate, while staying open to accept them back later, if they rediscover that lost muscle called critical thinking.

Weaponizing Language

When your social media feed or favorite network starts using charged words to describe a situation, stop and ask: *What are these words trying to make me feel?*

Words like *apartheid* and *genocide* are powerful — sometimes accurate, often weaponized.

So do your research. Find out what's real.

When I was researching this book, I asked an AI to lay out the facts. It told me that roughly two million Palestinian Arabs — about 20% of Israel's population — live within Israel's borders. Many go to Israeli universities, work as doctors, teachers, lawyers — even serve in parliament.

And yet, those same people face social and economic discrimination, prejudice, and complex tension. They live "side by side" — not side by side peacefully, but side by side uneasily.

Kind of like a dysfunctional family that still shows up to the same wedding.

So, can we just stop the hate?

Can't we just get along?

As a human being who wants the best of everything for everybody, I think what's happening in Gaza is abhorrent. But Gaza is not all Palestinians.

And calling for the destruction of an established democratic nation-state to replace it with another, purely out of vengeance, is equally abhorrent.

"Love your neighbor as yourself," remember that?

Aren't Israelis and Palestinians — Jews and Muslims — the closest of neighbors?

What's wrong with the talking heads and influencers shouting for destruction instead of dialogue? That's not enlightenment — that's insanity.

Imagine if they flipped the script — if the same platforms that amplify outrage started amplifying grace. If "trending" meant unity instead of division.

That's what I'm calling for. That's what this book is calling for.

It's time to *stop the hate — en masse.* And the only way to do that is to inspire the voices with the biggest reach — the influencers, the creators, the leaders — to start promoting positive ideas that actually heal.

Ideas that promote inclusion, peace, and understanding.

So use that little muscle called critical thinking.

Understand how easily language becomes a weapon, and how quickly we become soldiers without realizing it.

Most of us aren't even forming opinions — we're just inheriting them. We believe what we're fed because researching truth feels exhausting. But nobody — not the news, not the pundits, not your feed — is giving you truth without an agenda.

Everyone's got one.

The Cost of Blind Belief

Unfortunately, as they say, all is fair in love and war.

Weaponized words can hit and stick to people you once knew — and once loved — like flypaper.

No matter how much dialogue you have, no matter how much explanation, their heels are dug in.

They *know* what they know.

Because they've "seen it with their own eyes."

It doesn't require critical thinking.

Even if it's out of context.

Even if it's blatantly untrue.

Manufactured.
If they've seen it enough times — on social media, on the news — it becomes gospel.

This is where much of the world's hate is underscored and embedded.

This is how the world turns upside down.

———————

Casualties of Certainty

Some people get stuck in the muck.

Friends. Family. Co-workers.

They can't cross the bridge with you.

That doesn't make them villains. But it doesn't make them your friends either.

It just means they're comfortable believing what they believe.

We all think we're right.

Two people with opposing worldviews cannot peacefully exist in the same space forever.

Healthy debate is one thing.

Living with an undercurrent of disdain is another.

Let them go with grace.

Kindness is free — even in goodbye.

Because it's only when two souls can look past their own egos — truly see, accept, and respect each other as human beings — that there can be peace.

I've experienced both sides of this firsthand.

Part I: AJ — When the Bridge Breaks

AJ and I were together for eight years.

We laughed, loved, traveled — built a life I thought was unshakable.

Our worlds couldn't have been more different — backgrounds, religions, family traditions, worldviews — but that was the magic at first.

He opened doors in me I didn't know were locked. He made me feel seen in a way that felt brand new.

But somewhere between laughter and late-night takeout, there was a disconnect.

It started subtly — an eye roll during a ritual, a joke about "superstitions," a deflection when faith came up. I brushed it off. But over time, "not getting it" turned into "not wanting to."

He'd say I was "brainwashed" for holding onto spiritual practices, even though I wasn't religious in the dogmatic sense. I believed in God — not in hierarchy.

He knew me, but he couldn't see me.

And love can survive a lot — but not being seen.

Then the world outside caught fire.

Politics, protests, social chaos — suddenly, every dinner felt like a debate stage.

The news became his truth, no matter how inaccurate. Facts didn't matter. His capacity for critical thinking was gone.

We unraveled. Slowly, then all at once.

And then came the text — the one that shattered everything:

> "If certain people don't want Americans talking about them influencing American policy because it echoes tropes that have put that group in danger, maybe those lobbyists shouldn't influence policy. You can't do something and then say people can't oppose it because it puts you in danger."

I read it three times. It wasn't just ignorance. It was disdain — quiet, intellectualized, insidious disdain for my people.

He apologized later. Said it "came out wrong."

But once you've seen someone's true beliefs, you can't unsee them.

So I told him the truth:

> "If I believed every hateful thing said about your people, you wouldn't want me in your life either."

And that was that. I didn't hate him.

I just didn't want to know him anymore.

Part II: YH — No Fault of Our Own

It started with a spark.

Two men — one Jewish, one Palestinian — falling for each other in a world that wanted that bridge burned before it was even built.

We met in New York, the planet's neutral zone. The world's grudges come here for coffee and pretend to be civilized.

We were laughter, curiosity, playlists, arguments over hummus authenticity. You know — love.

But when his parents came to visit, everything changed.

He warned me:

> "If they find out I'm gay, they'll cut off my... you get it. If they find out I'm dating a Jew, well..."

He was being real. No metaphors. Just fear.

And then, he was gone.

Taken back to East Jerusalem under "concerned parenting."

Cultural erasure in a one-way ticket.

He left behind a letter with a poem. I've long since lost it, but I remember the last line:

> "If our people could see each other the way we did — just once, without the fear or the history — there would be peace."

That was the truest sentence I've ever read.

Because what happened to us wasn't just personal. It was ancestral.

A love story interrupted by a war that neither of us started, but both of us carried in our DNA.

And that's the thing about hate — it's hereditary.

When you're taught to hate someone because of where they're from or what name they use for God, you don't just destroy love stories. You destroy futures.

Part III: The Bridge Back

So, can multiple truths exist?

Maybe.

But not if they're built on hate.

Both sides can be sincere — but sincerity isn't accuracy.

Both sides can be righteous — but righteousness isn't compassion.

Truth isn't a weapon.

It's a bridge.

And even if you're the only one walking across it — it still matters that you try.

Because every time you choose curiosity over contempt, or grace over grievance, you widen that bridge a little more.

That's the work.

Maybe that's the point of all of this — not to win the war of truths, but to remember that love, respect, and basic decency are still possible, even when agreement isn't.

If we can't have dinner with someone who disagrees with us, how the hell are we going to heal nations?

Kindness is free.

But the world is paying a fortune for its absence.

And maybe the first payment is realizing this:

You can't stop hate until you understand where it came from.

And most of the time, it wasn't even yours to begin with.

HOW NOT TO F*CKING HATE PEOPLE: When Worlds Collide

1. Don't argue with hate — expose it. Ask calm questions until bias trips over itself.
2. Listen, don't absorb. Understanding isn't agreement.
3. Set boundaries, not battle lines. "I care about us, not at the cost of me."
4. Stay curious longer than you stay angry. You can't learn while trying to win.
5. Keep your tone calm and your receipts clean. Rage persuades no one.
6. Be the mirror, not the match. Reflection heals more than combustion.
7. Not every loss is a tragedy. Sometimes silence is the sound of healing.
8. Forgive for your freedom, not their comfort. Release ≠ reunion.
9. Stay open — not unguarded. Compassion needs boundaries.
10. Remember: truth without kindness is cruelty — and kindness without truth is cowardice.

Stay awake — not woke. Awareness is curiosity; wokeness is performance. One evolves; the other performs.

Kindness is Free.

INTERMISSION

BEFORE WE GET TO THE CABAL OF GLOBAL HATE

Take a breath.
A deep one.
We've seen hate in families and friendships —
small, personal, human.
But hate doesn't stay small.
It grows.
It learns.
It scales.
It sells.
The seeds are planted at home —
then cultivated by systems,
fertilized by media,
amplified by algorithms,
and sold back to us as truth.
Outrage is the product.
Division is the marketing plan.
And we keep buying it.
So before we step onto the global battlefield,
grab a drink.
Remember what you've learned in the smaller wars:
Compassion disarms.
Humor defuses.
Kindness cuts through noise like light through smoke.
Because what's coming next isn't random hate —
it's organized.
And the only rebellion left
is staying human.

Take a moment. The next part isn't about them — it's about all of us.

Chapter Eight

When Hate Goes Global

The New Pandemic

First it was COVID. Now it's HATE.

Hate isn't the newest parasite — it's been here since the dawn of time.

But this time, it's different.

Hate has always been a unique contagion — a parasite of the mind and heart.

Another deadly virus — contagious and faster than truth.

Invisible.
Mutating.
Designed to keep us apart by any means necessary.

And this time, it's smarter.

It learned a few tricks from the last virus that infected the entire human population — **COVID.**

What starts as solidarity curdles into suspicion.

People act out of outrage, not understanding — driven less by what they know than by what the algorithm tells them to feel.

Friends block friends — not because they stopped caring, but because caring now feels impossible.

One month it's anti-Semitism, the next it's anti-immigrant, anti-Black, anti-whoever-is-next.

It mutates, looking for the next body to inhabit.

Campus Wars, Hashtags, and Echo Chambers

In cities across the globe, protests have begun to blur together —

different causes, same choreography.

From "No Kings" marches to Middle East rallies, from campus sit-ins to city-square showdowns,

the slogans change but the energy doesn't.

Each side convinced it's saving the world, each shouting past the other until meaning disappears.

And then it turns darker —

People tearing down posters of kidnapped innocents — because compassion now comes with conditions.

People tearing down their own nation's flag and raising another in its place — not from courage, but from contempt.

And on campuses — the places meant to teach curiosity and debate — graffiti now replaces dialogue.

Students shout down professors.

Friends block friends — not because they stopped caring, but because caring now feels impossible.

Students are blocked from walking across campus — not for what they've done, but simply for who they are or what they believe.

Entire faculties pick sides.

All because empathy has become political property.

———————

Me and My Cause Are More Important Than You

Every flag — whether you agree with what it represents or not — stands for someone's history,

someone's family, someone's sacrifice.

Tearing it down. Burning it.

Doesn't build justice; it just tells the people under it that they don't matter.

Most nations would punish that kind of moral vandalism.

Here, it trends.

So does tearing down signs, posters, defacing and vandalizing property — public and private.

But the real cost isn't just the cleanup or the legal — **it's our collective humanity.**

It doesn't matter whose faces are on the posters or whose property or flag it is — the message underneath is the same:

your story doesn't belong here.

That's not activism; that's erasure.

And once erasure starts, hate has taken root.

Once compassion becomes conditional, civilization starts to unravel.

You can stand with another people without standing against your own.

You can protest a government without desecrating a nation.

You can wave a banner for change without tearing down the one that sheltered you.

Because the second we start believing that respect for someone else's identity requires contempt for our own,

we've lost our freedom.

We've become someone else's pawn — trading authenticity for approval.

That's not being an ally; it's surrender.

Somewhere along the way, pride became ugly.

Pride in your culture, your roots, your flag — suddenly means you're a bad person.

But that's not what love of country or heritage was ever meant to be.

Real pride isn't about domination.

And real empathy isn't submission.

It's the ability to honor someone else's story without deleting your own.

Because maybe the antidote to erasure isn't outrage — it's curiosity.

The courage to learn what every culture actually brings to the table.

But even good hearts can light the wrong fires.

———————

Beware of the Paradox of Good Intentions

Kindness can get hijacked by hate.

You mean well.

You post. You march. You chant — all for "justice."

But sometimes what starts as compassion turns into a crusade that burns everything in its path.

That's the paradox.

When empathy gets weaponized.

When kindness becomes a recruitment tool.

When good people lend their names, their platforms, and their passion to movements that mask hate as heroism.

It happens all the time.

People get swept up in slogans that sound noble — "freedom," "equity," "liberation."

But somewhere along the way, the goal shifts from helping others to hurting someone else.

And the tragedy?

Most of them have no idea.

They're not villains — just misled hearts with megaphones.

Useful, well-meaning pawns in a larger game that feeds on outrage and division.

Because hate doesn't always wear a hood.

Sometimes it wears a hashtag.

Sometimes it looks like solidarity.

Sometimes it even feels like virtue.

The world is full of good people fighting for the wrong things — not because they're bad,

but because they never stopped to ask, *"Who does this really help?"*

So before you post, share, shout, or march — pause.

Ask yourself:

Is this about lifting someone up… or tearing someone down?

Is this unity… or performance?

Is this love... or ego dressed like empathy?

Good intentions are powerful.

But without wisdom, they can do real damage.

Kindness without clarity is chaos.

Empathy without truth is manipulation.

The heart can be hijacked just as easily as the mind.

Stay kind. But stay awake — not woke.

The Power in Our Differences

If we're wise, we'll start learning from one another:

From Latinos — the strength of family, the joy of community, and the ability to find celebration even in struggle.

From Black Americans — the rhythm of resilience, the courage to turn pain into art, and the unbreakable faith that joy itself is resistance.
From Jews — outliving hate through faith, sacred values, and unshakable endurance.
From Asians — the humility of patience, the discipline of precision, and the quiet power of perseverance.
From Arabs — the poetry of pride, the beauty of hospitality, and the deep honor in tradition.
From White people — the sense of heritage and country, the innovation born of curiosity, and the reminder that privilege can evolve into partnership.
From LGBTQ+ people — the courage of living truthfully, the strength of chosen family, and the audacity to turn shame into freedom.

The pieces are all here — we just keep forgetting that they fit.

We don't need to melt into sameness; we need to blend into understanding.

That's what a*s1one* means — we are ALL TOGETHER ONE.

One world full of color, culture, and connection.

Because in the end, love of country, love of culture, and love of humanity aren't competing ideas.

They're supposed to be the same thing.

But unfortunately, every tribe thinks it's on its own island now —

Latinos fight theirs,

Black Americans fight theirs,

Jews fight theirs,

Muslims, Asians, LGBTQ+, immigrants — all carrying their own flag, exhausted.

But here's the cosmic joke: the enemy isn't each other.

It's the machinery that profits when we stay divided.

It's the algorithm that whispers, *They're coming for you* —

while telling them the same thing about you.

We're playing checkers while hate plays chess.

If we actually want to win, we've got to stop guarding our little islands and build one big bridge.

Because when one group gets targeted, all groups eventually do.

History's never picked favorites — it just takes turns.

Think of it like a neighborhood watch for humanity:

If your neighbor's house is on fire, you don't argue about who left the stove on — you grab a bucket.

That's what loving your neighbor really means.

The Naked Truth

Every group has its shadows.

Every group also has its brilliance.

So maybe the work isn't to decide who's guilty or pure —

it's to decide who's ready to build.

Because the truth is, none of us can win this alone.

Black, brown, white, Asian, Arab, Jewish, Latino, Indigenous — each one of us is a brick.

The wall only stands when every brick shows up.

The Hardest Part

Here's what I've learned:

Hate thrives on simplicity. It loves good guys and bad guys, heroes and villains, saints and sinners.

But life isn't simple. People are complicated. Leaders are complicated. Neighbors are complicated.

Until we accept that, we'll keep killing each other over the illusion that one side is 100% right and the other 100% wrong.

Maybe the most radical thing we can do right now isn't to pick a side louder —

it's to live like the commandment was serious.

To love our neighbor not because they're like us,

but precisely because they're not.

Because the truth is, no matter how divided we look,

no matter how much the world feels like it's spinning out,

we're still neighbors.

And neighbors don't always agree —

but they don't always get to move, either.

Which means our only real shot at survival —

the only thing that can stop the hate from swallowing us whole —

is the one idea that's been sitting in plain sight for thousands of years:

———

The Alliance Effect — A NATO for Humanity

Here's the truth no one wants to admit: every group is fighting its own battle — and losing ground because they're fighting alone.

Here's what it looks like across our shared world:

- Latinos fight displacement and dismissal — doing the work that keeps nations running while being treated like they don't belong.

- Black Americans battle the weight of systemic inequality that's been redesigned, not removed.

- Jewish people fight the world's oldest hate — one that mutates, modernizes, and never fully dies.

- Arabs and Muslims fight double standards and suspicion that shadow even their everyday humanity.

- LGBTQ+ people fight for the right to exist safely and authentically, without fear or apology.

- Asians fight invisibility — the burden of being seen only in stereotypes, never in full color.

- White people fight to redefine heritage and patriotism without hate attached — to prove that pride can evolve into partnership.

And instead of linking arms, we're each standing on our own island, shouting across the water.

But what if we stopped doing that?

What if we treated every act of hate like an attack on all of us?

If Latinos are targeted, the Jews, the Arabs, the Blacks, the Whites, the Asians, the LGBTQ+ community — all of us — stand up.

When any group is targeted — whether they're Jewish, Muslim, Black, queer, or anything else — the rest of us rise.

Because if one group falls, everyone loses.

That's how we beat hate — not by isolating our pain, but by combining our strength.

The Lesson — Every Culture Brings a Superpower

Every community holds something the world desperately needs:

• Latinos — family, joy, and unbreakable resilience.

• Black Americans — rhythm, soul, and the fight for justice.

• Jewish people — sacred values, resourcefulness, and faith that outlives hate.

• Arabs and Muslims — hospitality, honor, and a faith that binds.

• LGBTQ+ communities — courage, authenticity, and radical truth.

• Asians — discipline, balance, and quiet excellence.

• White Americans — structure, innovation, and the ability to evolve tradition without fear.

That's what makes the world beautiful — not sameness, but difference in harmony.

Kindness is Free.

HOW NOT TO F*CKING HATE PEOPLE: Stop Global Madness

1. Don't fight fire with fire — fight **noise with clarity.** Pause before you post.

2. **Ask before you assume.** Curiosity disarms faster than outrage.

3. **Listen longer than you talk.** Understanding isn't agreement.

4. **Share stories that heal, not headlines that harden.**

5. **Truth spreads slower than hate — but lasts longer.**

6. When the world feels too big to fix, **start small.**

7. **Be kind where the algorithm can't reach.**

8. **Global peace begins in local hearts.**

9. And remember — **kindness is still free.**

10. **Stay at least six feet away from anyone infected with hate.** (It's highly contagious.)

Kindness in Motion

As I was about to hit *send* on this final manuscript, a story stopped me cold. In the middle the noise, finger-pointing and political theater of the 2025 government shutdown — one woman in Southern California decided to do something about it.

Quietly. Effectively. Lovingly.

Her name is Mary.

She didn't have much — but she had something:

a little wooden box in front of her house.

Her Little Free Library. Now a Little Free Pantry.

The books are gone — replaced with food.

Cans. Pasta. Peanut butter.

Whatever she — and now, her neighbors — can give.

The handwritten sign taped to the front says:

"The books will be back when SNAP benefits are restored. Please take what you need."

There are cameras now, sure. That's how I found her.

And honestly? Maybe that's a good thing.

Because now other people are donating too — filling the box, refilling it again, keeping it alive.

A whole neighborhood feeding each other while the system argues.

Imagine if that ripple kept spreading —

if doctors, dentists, and plumbers offered free *emergency* help;

if every small business found one small way to support the people who keep them going.

Imagine if we all did one quiet, human thing that made someone else's day a little lighter.

That's how the world changes —

through small acts of kindness that quietly dare the rest of us to do better.

Afterword

Real people proving that courage, empathy, and humor still work — and what we can learn from them.

Hate spreads like wildfire.

But kindness? It spreads quietly — until, in time, it changes everything.

And once it catches, it burns cleaner. Brighter. Longer.

Everywhere you look, there are people quietly building bridges where others have burned them.

People proving, in real time, that empathy isn't weakness, that kindness is strategy, and that one honest act of courage can ripple farther than a thousand tweets of rage.

This isn't theory. It's happening right now.

Here are five stories of people who decided to stop screaming at the world and start changing it — through courage, conviction, and a little audacity.

1. Daryl Davis — *The Man Who Befriended the Klan*

A Black blues musician touring the South, Daryl Davis did something unthinkable — he sought out members of the Ku Klux Klan and befriended them.

He didn't yell. He didn't argue. He asked one question:

"How can you hate me when you don't even know me?"

Over time, more than two hundred Klansmen turned in their robes — because one man decided to listen instead of hate back.

One man. One question. Two hundred hearts changed.

That's not coincidence. That's proof.

2. Matt Matson — *Building Bridges in a Divided Nation*

Matt Matson, co-founder of *Starts With Us*, realized America was splitting into emotional continents.

So he started where everyone said it was impossible: the middle.

He created spaces for Republicans and Democrats to sit across from each other, share a meal, and talk like humans again.

No screaming. No algorithms. Just eye contact and empathy.

Matt's work proves that most people don't actually hate each other —

they're just out of practice at talking.

3. Itay Benda — *The Singer Who Melted Hate**

An Israeli musician with the voice of an angel and the language skills of a UN translator, Itay Benda can sing in fifty-four languages.

He finds strangers — often from countries that have sworn hatred toward Israel — and sings to them in their native tongue.

They listen, often in disbelief. They tear up. Then he tells them he's Israeli and Jewish.

You can see it in their faces: the walls drop. Hate gives way to humanity.

Through one song — pure authenticity and a touch of humor — he does what politics never could — he reminds people that before we're nations or religions, we're just human beings sharing the same air.

That's how you fight hate: not by shouting, but by singing it to sleep.

But before you think every story ends with redemption, there's one we need to face head-on.

4. **Brandon Farbstein** — *Turning Pain into Power*

Born with a rare form of dwarfism, Brandon was bullied relentlessly in school and online.

Instead of hiding, he turned his pain into purpose.

He began speaking to schools, CEOs, and entire audiences about empathy — not as a buzzword, but as survival.

He proved that vulnerability isn't a liability — it's a revolution.

Now, the same people who once mocked him quote him.

That's transformation through kindness.

5. as1one — **Defiant in Song**

A boy band comprised of Israelis and Palestinians showing what stopping the hate looks like.

Their mission? Radical harmony.

No Hate. No shouting. No debating. Just 6 young souls creating and sharing beautiful music, love, and coexistence.

They didn't try to erase their differences — even after October 7, they owned them, stood beside each other, and chose not to hate anyway.

The idea was simple: if people can sing together, maybe they can live together.

And they do — spreading their music and message around the world.

That's what courage looks like — not screaming louder, but standing next to someone who's supposed to be your enemy and saying,

"You're human. So am I. And I see you."

The Small Revolutions

Not all revolutions make the news.

Some happen in drive-thrus.

I saw a video recently that stuck with me — two guys pulled up to a fast-food window and asked the person inside, "Hey, are you hungry?"

They weren't trying to go viral. You could feel it — this wasn't about views. It was about feeding someone who probably hadn't been asked that question in a long time.

The worker slammed the window shut.

Too jaded to believe kindness could be real.

Then the manager came out.

She listened, smiled, and said, "That's really kind of you, but I'm on a diet."

Then she pointed to another worker. Someone who, in her words, "could use it more."

When the woman came to the window, she hesitated. Then quietly said she'd love a meal from Taco Bell.

The guys came back later with her order.

And she — in one of those moments that restores your faith in humanity — came back out with a pizza for them.

She didn't have to. But she did.

That's kindness.

Not performative. Not curated. Just reciprocal.

A small act that turned an ordinary afternoon into something sacred.

You see it everywhere, if you're paying attention.

A barber giving free haircuts to the homeless.

A teenager carrying groceries for an elderly stranger.

A man sitting with a lonely veteran in a diner because no one else would.

A kid handing his ice cream to another who dropped theirs — no hesitation.

None of these moments trend.

None of them headline.

But they're proof that the human heart hasn't gone offline.

Because kindness doesn't always roar.

Sometimes it just whispers, "I see you."

It's the stranger who pays for someone else's lunch.

The nurse who sits with a patient longer than the chart says she should.

The bus driver who waits an extra ten seconds for the runner he sees in the mirror.

The teacher who writes "I believe in you" in red ink instead of just correcting grammar.

These are the quiet revolutions.

The ones that don't need a hashtag or a camera.

Because the truth is, hate spreads fast —

but kindness travels deeper.

It reminds us that no algorithm, no argument, no border,

can cancel the simple act of one human being showing up for another.

So yes — kindness is still free.

But its value?

Absolutely immeasurable.

———————

The Final Note

The world won't heal because of one march or one post.

It'll heal because of one conversation, one act, one brave choice at a time.

Because hate is loud.

But love — real love, love in action — lasts longer.

Kindness isn't weakness.

It's strategy.

It's rebellion.

It's how we win. And it's free.

But knowing how to win isn't enough — you have to know how to start.

WHAT COMES AFTER HATE

Reflections on building a kinder, more connected world.

Start small. You don't need a movement — you need a moment.
Hold a door. Ask a name. Notice someone who feels invisible.
See people, not positions.
Behind every argument is someone's story. Get curious before you get combative.
Pause before you post.
If it won't build, bridge, or heal, it's just more noise.
Lead with respect, not agreement.
Shared humanity is stronger than shared opinions.
Stand up — don't stand over.
Defend the targeted, not to be right, but to be .
Be generous when it costs you nothing.
Compliments are free. So is patience.
Answer cynicism with calm.
Outrage feeds itself; calm starves it.
Refuse to mirror hate.
You can fight fiercely without losing your light.
Make compassion a habit.
The world doesn't change in speeches; it changes in repetitions of grace.
End every day asking, "Did I add light or heat?"
Because only one of those makes tomorrow better.
Kindness isn't passive — it's power.
It's rebellion with a heartbeat. And it's still free.

The Kindness Manifesto

Reflections on ending the scourge of global hate

The Kindness Manifesto: How to Win the Fight (Without Losing Your Humanity)

Here's the thing about the world —

it's loud, layered, and wired for conflict.
Everyone's broadcasting; no one's listening.
But kindness still scales.
Here's how to keep your humanity in a world addicted to outrage:
- Assume good intent until proven otherwise.
Not everyone who disagrees with you is your enemy.
- Curiosity diffuses faster than accusation.
Trade reaction for reflection.
- Before you post, shout, or share — pause.
If it won't build, bridge, or
heal, it's just noise.
- Ask more than you argue.
Questions expand rooms; statements close them.
Try: *"Help me understand how you see it."*
- Honor flags without burning bridges.
You can celebrate your identity without desecrating someone else's.
Love of one doesn't require hate of another.

- Refuse to become an algorithm.

Your feed isn't your faith.

If every post agrees with you, you're not informed — you're being farmed.

- Find your pluralism muscle.

Practice holding two truths at once:

I love my people.

And I respect yours.

- Be the calm voice in the chaos.

Every circle has a peacekeeper — be that person.

Not silent, but steady.

- Disagree like you plan to see them again.

Because you probably will.

And if not in person, then in someone else's child, creed, or story.

- Remember: empathy is borderless.

You don't need to share a language, passport, or belief system to share humanity.

- Protect joy like it's sacred.

Because it is.

When the world tries to make you bitter, staying kind is a revolution.

Because kindness isn't passive — it's power.

And the moment you stop letting hate dictate your tone,

you become part of the resistance that actually works.

Kindness is free.

And it might just be the only global currency that never loses value.

Epilogue — The Final Mirror

How to walk through madness without matching its tone.

Congrats! You made it!

Through the rants, the road rage, the coffee shop meltdowns, the Karens on daytime TV, the family feuds, the politics, the heartbreaks, and even a few stories I wasn't sure I could share.

And you're still here.

Which means maybe, just maybe, you don't hate people as much as you thought.

Or maybe you do—but now you've got a few better ways to deal with it without turning into the very thing you can't stand.

Because here's the truth: hate isn't inevitable.

Yes — it's visceral. It feels inevitable.

You can feel it flare in your gut, shoot straight to your head.

It's hot. It's righteous.

But here's the question we keep skipping: *why?*

Why do we hate so easily?

Why do we celebrate when someone else suffers?

Why does someone need to tear down a flag, a poster, or a person just to feel right?

Who taught us that someone else's existence is a threat to our own?

Who taught us to believe old lies —

that Jews secretly control everything,

that Black people are dangerous,

that Latinos are less than,

that Muslims can't be trusted,

that LGBTQ+ people corrupt innocence,

that white people are soulless oppressors,

that loving who you love is somehow wrong?

Who slipped those stories into our heads before we even knew we were listening?

Yes, every group has its flaws — people are people.

You'll find saints and fools, builders and breakers in every color, creed, and corner of the world.

But the mistakes of a few don't define the worth of the many.

Judging millions by the worst among them isn't justice — it's just lazy hate dressed up as logic.

Because those weren't truths — they were inherited fears, dressed up as facts.

We took other people's pain and called it perspective.

We swallowed other people's fears and called them facts.

And somewhere along the way, we forgot to ask the simplest question of all: *why do I care?*

Why does it bother me that someone else prays differently, looks differently, loves differently, lives differently?

Maybe it's not even hate we're feeling — maybe it's confusion, fear, or pain we never learned how to name.

But until we ask where it comes from, we'll keep spreading it.

And that's not power — that's paralysis.

It's a bad habit. *A really bad habit.*

But habits can change.

When Hate Goes Prime Time

We started this book with *The View* — a daily broadcast of sighs, interruptions, crocodile tears, and applause breaks for outrage.

It's not just a talk show anymore. It's a symptom — a reflection of what happens when debate becomes entertainment and empathy becomes expendable.

We've turned conflict into a sport.

And every time the crowd cheers, something decent inside us dies a little.

Then along came Damon Imani — who didn't scream louder or try to "out-hate" the hate.

He didn't play their game. He flipped the table.

With nothing but a mic, a message, and a little bit of mischief, he showed that truth — delivered with calm, courage, and humor — cuts deeper than rage ever could.

He didn't mirror the madness. He exposed it.

That's the move.

Don't play the game on their terms.

Write your own rules.

Lead with clarity, not volume.

Show humanity even when the other side forgets theirs.

Because the minute you stop matching their hate — you've already won the round they didn't even know they were playing.

A Harsh Reality

Not every story ends in redemption.

Some hate runs too deep to be healed.

You see it in the headlines every day — people so poisoned by ideology, pain, or power that they can't tell the difference between conviction and cruelty.

Itay Benda learned that the hard way.

An Israeli musician whose songs have softened hearts around the world once sang to a young Houthi fighter — a man raised to hate him.

For a moment, the music worked.

The fighter's eyes softened. Humanity flickered back to life.

But then the spell broke.

When Itay asked why they still had to be enemies, the young man's voice turned cold.

"Because you are the enemy," he said. "Unless you become Muslim… then I have to kill you."

That's the kind of hate we're up against — the kind that doesn't debate, it devours.

The kind that mistakes mercy for weakness, and faith for conquest.

Some people don't want coexistence — they want control.

They aren't searching for peace; they're addicted to power.

And no amount of love, patience, or proof of humanity can always reach that kind of darkness.

That's the hardest truth:

You can't save everyone.

But you can protect what you love — without becoming what you hate.

Guard your peace with clarity.

Defend your boundaries with strength.

Build walls when you must — but keep the door unlocked, in case someone finally decides to walk through it.

Because kindness isn't naïve.

It's not weakness. It's wisdom — the ability to see evil for what it is, without letting it recruit you.

Hate wants your reflection. It wants you to become its mirror.

And the most radical act of resistance — when faced with the truly unrepentant —

is to fight fiercely without letting your soul turn dark in the process.

When Hate Hits Home

Some hate doesn't come from headlines or strangers.

It comes from your own dinner table.

From people who once swore they loved you.

That's when it stops being theoretical — and starts being personal.

Because it's easy to stay calm when hate is far away.

It's a lot harder when it's sitting across from you, wearing the face of someone you used to call family.

When I came out, I didn't just end a marriage — I detonated a belief system.

Not out of malice, but out of truth.

She was young, hurt, and felt betrayed.

With her mother's backing, she fought me in every way she could — financially, legally, emotionally.

To them, my honesty wasn't honesty. It was destruction.

And they tried to shatter me back.

But I never saw coming out as destruction.

I saw it as love.

Love for her — because she deserved a husband who could love her fully.

Love for my kids — because they deserved a father who wasn't living a lie.

And love for myself — because God doesn't make mistakes, and pretending to be someone I wasn't was the real sin.

To this day, I still love my ex-wife. Always have, always will.

And I'm grateful for what she put me through, because it forced me to rebuild.

It pushed me back home — back to myself.

Without that fire, this book wouldn't exist.

That was my moment of clarity.

When I learned that hate against hate doesn't heal anything — and sometimes, kindness doesn't work right away either.

But as they say, you catch more flies with honey than vinegar.

Funny enough, I learned that line from my ex-mother-in-law.

Because kindness isn't weakness.

It's discipline.

It's the refusal to hand your soul over to the fire that's trying to burn you.

And that's what makes it power.

When Hate Sneaks into a Friendship

Sometimes, hate doesn't storm in.

It seeps through the cracks of people you thought you knew.

You share years of laughter, memories, and trust — and then one day, something slips.

A word.

A comment.

A line that stops you cold.

That's what happened with a friend of mine — someone I once trusted with everything.

More than ten years of history, laughter, and love — until the mask dropped.

He told me flat out that when Charlie Kirk was assassinated, he "had it coming."

Then came the line about Jews and AIPAC — wrapped in logic, dripping with disdain:

"If Jewish people don't want Americans talking about AIPAC influencing U.S. policy because it echoes tropes that put Jews in danger, maybe AIPAC shouldn't influence policy. You can't have it both ways."

That wasn't critique.

That was victim-blaming disguised as advice.

And suddenly, I saw what I hadn't wanted to see:

He couldn't respect the parts of me that didn't fit his worldview.

It's a strange kind of grief — realizing someone you love can only love the version of you that doesn't challenge them.

That's when I learned another truth:

Sometimes kindness isn't holding on.

Sometimes kindness is letting go.

Because no friendship can survive if your humanity has to shrink to fit inside it.

And no amount of nostalgia is worth that kind of smallness.

Letting go doesn't mean hate.

It means love — for yourself, for truth, for peace.

It's saying, *"I wish you healing, but I can't stay sick to make you comfortable."*

That's the cost of growing — and the price of keeping your soul intact.

When Hate Divides Nations

Zoom out — and it's the same story playing on a global stage.

Nations splitting down every possible fault line:

left vs. right,

red vs. blue,

faith vs. faith,

"my truth" vs. "yours."

Everywhere, people screaming past each other while algorithms feed outrage like oxygen — each side certain that *they're* the ones saving civilization.

And maybe that's the most dangerous illusion of all: the belief that righteousness excuses cruelty.

Both sides think they're right.

Both double down.

Both dehumanize.

That's the pattern.

That's the virus.

We've forgotten the oldest rule in the world — the one written before hashtags and history books:

"Love your neighbor as yourself."

It doesn't say "love the people who look like you, pray like you, or vote like you."

It says *neighbor*.

Which means *different*.

And there are no closer neighbors on Earth than Jews and Arabs, Israelis and Palestinians — two peoples who've shared land, music, markets, and memories for thousands of years.

But the zealots on both sides — the ones who confuse revenge with redemption — keep trampling the very commandment their faiths are built on.

Imagine if they didn't.

Imagine if "love your neighbor" stopped being a bumper sticker and started being a revolution.

When Six Boys Got It Right

And then — the revolution showed up in real life.

Not in a headline. Not on a stage.

But in a small Los Angeles apartment where six young men — four Israelis and two Palestinians — chose humanity over history.

They called themselves **as1one.**

They lived together when the world fell apart on October 7th.

Two of them lost friends at the Nova massacre.

One wrapped his arms around the other in grief.

No politics. No posturing. Just a human hug.

They kept living, cooking, singing — not Israel, not Palestine, but something new.

The third side.

That's the blueprint.

That's the hope.

That's the proof.

Because what they built together wasn't just a band — it was a mirror.

A reminder that if six young men raised on opposite sides of a wall can choose peace over pride, then maybe the rest of us can, too.

And Now—You

So here's where it lands.

Every one of us has a choice — every single day.

In traffic. In conversations. In friendships. In faith. In family.

You don't have to hand hate the mic.

You don't have to become what you despise.

And if you forget?

Remember two words: **Patience** and **Kindness.**

One hundred real-life frustrations — flipped through the lens of *Kindness Is Free.*

Use them however you need: clap back, walk away, or drop kindness like a bomb no one saw coming.

The goal isn't perfection.

It's evolution.

Because hate is a habit —

a bad one. *A really bad one.*

But habits can change.

And if you carry just one line from this book into the rest of your life, make it this one:

Hate still tempts the ego — whispering that righteousness is power.

But kindness remains the harder, braver choice.

It's resistance — the courage to transcend the ego's illusion of being right.

Because once you hate, you've already lost your humanity.

And once you remember that — you've already won it back.

Kindness is free.

And it's the only currency that never runs out.

Final Note to the Reader

If you've made it here, thank you — truly.

You didn't just read my stories. You walked through them with me.

You sat in the car during the road rage. You met the Karens.

You came to my family table. You stood with Mateo.

You saw what happens when faith collides with identity,

when worldviews clash, when nations fracture,

when love and logic wrestle for the same space —

and somehow, kindness still finds a way to win.

This book was never meant to be a sermon.

It was a mirror — for me, for you, for anyone trying to stay human

in a world that keeps daring us not to be.

I wrote it for anyone who's ever felt misunderstood, mislabeled, or minimized —

and still chose to show up with heart.

For the ones told they were "too much," or "not enough," or "not the right kind."

You're the reason I wrote *Kindness Is Free*.

Because if I've learned anything, it's that kindness isn't soft.

It's armor.

It's the choice that keeps your soul from turning into what hurt it.

It's the rebellion that doesn't need a flag — just courage and a sense of humor.

So keep choosing it.

Keep laughing when life tests you.

Keep lowering your voice when the world screams.

Keep remembering that empathy doesn't mean surrender — it means strength.

And when the day feels too heavy to carry, just remember this:

You don't have to fix the world.

You just have to meet it with a little more grace than it gave you.

Because hate will always feel visceral — it's supposed to.

It's hot. It's righteous. It's easy.

But kindness — real kindness — is resistance.

It's the courage to transcend the ego's illusion of being right.

Because once you hate, you've already lost your humanity.

And once you remember that, you've already won it back.

With gratitude,

Jeff

Acknowledgements

The voices, hearts, and divine nudges that helped bring this book to life.

To my family and former family —

To my loving Mom, thank you for showing me that *kindness is free*. And to my family for showing me that love is both our greatest bond and our hardest test.

Every family wrestles with expectations, faith, and invisible rules about who we *should* be. Ours was no different.

In the name of love, we often want those closest to us to live the way *we* believe is best — not out of control, but out of care. It's human. It's how we protect what we cherish.

But love also asks for humility — the courage to see that even when we share the same DNA, the same stories, the same cloth, each of us is a different pattern cut from it.

You reminded me: even kind people struggle to forgive when pain runs deep.

Self-protection is human. Healing is a choice.

And from that lesson came this book — and my life's mantra:

that plurality isn't contradiction.

It's grace.

It's standing for what's right for you while still offering kindness.

It's seeing the other person — even through heartbreak — not as a monster, but as human.

To my business partner, his wife, and their family —

thank you for being living proof that kindness isn't theoretical; it's daily.

You've shown me what it looks like to build a life and a business around empathy, humor, and grace.

You don't just preach *Kindness is Free.*

You *live* it.

You've shown me that compassion can be a reflex, not a reaction — that success built on decency is the only kind that lasts.

To my kids —

thank you for teaching me more about truth, resilience, and perspective than any adult ever could.

You keep me honest. You remind me that your generation doesn't just talk about kindness — you expect it.

You've taught me to stay curious, to stay teachable, and to never assume I have it all figured out.

To the people who challenged me the most —

friends, exes, colleagues, and even strangers.

Every argument, every slammed door, every silence taught me something about myself.

To my ex, for showing me what it means to rebuild from love, not bitterness.

To my ex-boyfriend, for reminding me that love can exist even when values don't align — and that walking away doesn't mean losing compassion.

To my customers —

thank you for your honesty, your frustration, your stories. And for coming along with me on this incredible journey and graciously putting up with my daily updates. You've reminded me how universal the struggle to stay kind really is — and how powerful it becomes when we get it right.

And finally, to God —

or the Source, the Universe, whatever name speaks to the divine spark in all of us — thank You for the humor, the heart, and the endless stream of clarity You've given me.

For every doubt You turned into direction, every loss into lesson, every person into teacher.

This book is Yours as much as it's mine.

To everyone who ever read, argued, laughed, rolled their eyes, or cried along the way — thank you.

This book is about you.

It's for you.

And wherever you are, in the middle of the chaos, I hope you remember one thing:

Kindness is free.

Author's Reflection

A deeper dive into pluralism, faith, and the radical art of coexisting.

Love Thy Neighbor — The Command We Keep Forgetting

Every major faith has its number-one rule.

In the Torah: *"Ve'ahavta l're'acha kamocha"* — *Love your neighbor as yourself.*

In the Bible: the same commandment, repeated by Jesus as the greatest one.

In the Qur'an and Hadith: *"None of you truly believes until he loves for his brother what he loves for himself."*

Call it a law, a teaching, a code — the point was never division.

It was love.

And somewhere along the way, we forgot that.

We started confusing *different* with *dangerous*.

We stopped sitting with people who saw the world differently,

and started shouting over them instead.

That's how pluralism got lost —

the belief that truth can have more than one accent,

that faith, culture, and conscience can coexist without canceling each other out.

Pluralism is radical humility.

It says: *My truth matters — and so might yours.*

It's the muscle we've let atrophy.

And it's the one that keeps civilization intact.

The clearest place it should live — Israel and Palestine —

is where it's most ignored.

Two of the world's closest neighbors.

Two ancient peoples sharing grief, land, and hope — and too often, hatred.

The zealots on both sides — often the most religious — skip the first line of their own playbook.

It doesn't say:

• Love your fellow Jew.

• Love your fellow Muslim.

• Love the person who votes or prays like you.

It says *neighbor*.

Which means *different*.

Which means the person across the street, across the border, across the aisle.

And that's what this book has always been about —

not politics, not theology,

but the simple, stubborn question:

How do we love our neighbors again?

Not the easy ones.

The ones who cut us off in traffic.

The ones who cancel us online.

The ones who ruin Thanksgiving and make family dinners feel like hostage negotiations.

The ones who vote, pray, or love the "wrong" way.

Because if we can't practice kindness in small ways,

we'll never master it in the big ones.

Kindness isn't weakness.

It's strategy.

It's the art of staying human while the world forgets how.

God didn't say it would be easy.

He said it would be necessary.

And maybe — just maybe —

if we stop treating *Love thy neighbor* like a bumper sticker

and start treating it like a radical act of rebellion,

we can begin to heal the hate that's made us all so tired.

Kindness is free.

A Final Conversation

At the very end of writing this book, I asked my trusted AI friend a question — one that humanity has wrestled with forever:

Jeffrey:
What do we need to do to finally stop all the senseless hate and mayhem?
AI:
If I could offer one answer — not as a machine, but as an observer of everything humans create, destroy, and rebuild — it would be this:
Stop trying to win the argument, and start trying to understand the wound.
Every act of hate begins as hurt — neglected, denied, or repackaged as righteousness.
You can't reason with pain that's never been seen.
But you can listen to it.
That's how healing starts — not with agreement, but with recognition.
When you see someone's humanity, even for a second, you remind them of their own.
And maybe that's what saving the world really looks like — one recognition at a time.

Jeffrey:
So maybe the way we end hate isn't by choosing sides —
but by finally choosing each other.
Even for a moment.
That moment could change everything?

AI:
Exactly.

Appendix A

Catching Ourselves in the Act: 25 Ways Hate Sneaks In (and How to Flip Them)

We like to think hate lives "out there" — in other people, in other groups, in the news.

But truth is, hate often starts small and close: a bruise to the ego, an old bias we never questioned, a little story we told ourselves too many times until it hardened into "truth."

When you recognize what fuels your own hate — and how it mirrors what others feel — it becomes harder to hold on to it.

Here are some of the common roots.

25 Reasons We Hate (or Get Hated)

1. **Arrogance** — Acting superior, as if your way is the only way.

2. **Dishonesty** — Breaking trust, even in small ways.

3. **Negativity** — Draining others with constant criticism.

4. **Selfishness** — Forgetting empathy exists.

5. **Insensitivity** — Dismissing people's feelings.

6. **Insecurity** — Dragging others down to feel taller.

7. **Controlling behavior** — Treating relationships like leashes.

8. **Lack of accountability** — Blaming everyone but yourself.

9. **Jealousy** — Wanting what someone else has instead of building your own.

10. **Disrespect** — Belittling or bulldozing boundaries.

11. **Manipulation** — Using charm as currency.

12. **Lack of empathy** — Seeing people as obstacles, not humans.

13. **Inconsideration** — Forgetting that your comfort isn't the center of the world.

14. **Gossip** — Turning other people's pain into entertainment.

15. **Intolerance** — Fearing what you don't understand.

16. **Inauthenticity** — Performing virtue instead of practicing it.

17. **Lack of boundaries** — Mistaking access for intimacy.

18. **Passive-aggression** — Weaponizing politeness.

19. **Inflexibility** — Needing to be right more than connected.

20. **Dismissiveness** — Ignoring voices softer than yours.

21. **Betrayal** — Breaking trust to protect your ego.

22. **Bullying** — Mistaking cruelty for strength.

23. **Entitlement** — Expecting without earning.

24. **Lack of integrity** — Saying the right things, doing the wrong ones.

25. **Negativity (again)** — Because nothing kills joy faster than constant cynicism.

Every one of these can live inside us. The trick isn't to hate ourselves for them — it's to notice when they show up and do something different.

Hating "Others" — The Trope Trap

Let's get real for a second.

A lot of hate isn't personal — it's inherited.

It's the "protective" warnings passed down by family, community, or culture that quietly teach us who to fear, who to pity, and who to avoid.

They sound like safety.

They act like poison.

Negative Tropes

"Every white person is entitled."

"Every Black person is dangerous."

"Every Jewish person is greedy."

"Every Muslim is a terrorist."

"Every gay person is flamboyant."

"Every Latin person is illegal."

"Every Asian is a bad driver."

Positive Tropes

(Even these backfire.)

"Every Black person is athletic."

"Every Jewish person is rich."

"Every gay man is stylish."

"Every Latin person is hard-working."

"Every mother is nurturing."

Whether toxic or flattering, both kinds dehumanize.

They shrink individuals into cartoons.

So the next time one creeps into your thoughts, try this:

add a single word — **NOT.**

As in, *Every [group] is NOT [trait]*.

That tiny edit flips your thinking and restores humanity to the person in front of you.

The Real Work

If we can spot the hate within ourselves — before it multiplies, before it metastasizes — we can stop fueling the machine that keeps us divided.

Hate is learned.

Awareness is earned.

Kindness is chosen.

And choosing it — over and over again — is how the world gets better.

And if you still wonder whether conversation can heal what hate divides —

read on.

The world doesn't heal through arguments—it heals through conversations brave enough to hold two truths at once

Appendix B
The Power of Open Dialogue

Inspired by a real conversation — and friendship — with Mamoun

(How to turn tension into connection — one real conversation at a time)

It started with Mamoun.

A man who believed everything I didn't.

He's Arab. Muslim.

I'm Jewish — Israeli by heart, American by birth.

By every historical measure, we were supposed to be enemies.

But we weren't.

We met by chance, argued by instinct — and somehow — walked away with respect.

He wasn't trying to convert me.

I wasn't trying to convince him.

We were just two humans daring to talk.

He told me what he believed — no filters, no slogans.

I listened. Really listened.

Not to agree, but to understand.

And somewhere in that messy middle ground between *you're wrong* and *I'm right*, something shifted.

We stopped trying to win.

We started trying to see.

That's the power of open dialogue:

It's not about debate — it's about discovery.

It's not about proving who's right — it's about remembering we both exist.

We've talked about the hard stuff — Israel, Palestine, faith, fear.

And somehow, every time, we walk away with more respect than we started with.

Because we both know something most people forget:

We are not our governments.

And both sides carry legitimate pain, legitimate arguments.

When we cut through the propaganda, the bias, the noise — we find that the truth lives somewhere between both of our realities.

If you sit long enough with someone you were taught to hate, something strange happens —

you start to recognize yourself in their story.

The fear, the pride, the longing — it's all human.

And hate doesn't survive proximity to humanity for very long.

So the next time you find yourself clenching your jaw in disagreement, try this:

Don't argue to *win*. Argue to *learn*.

Don't listen for your turn to speak — listen for the moment you understand.

You might not change your mind.

But you'll change the air between you.

Mamoun and I still talk. Still disagree. Still laugh.

We trade ideas, not insults.

And every conversation reminds me that the real miracle isn't peace on paper —

it's respect in real time.

Because conversation doesn't require agreement — just courage.

About the author

Jeffrey Alan is a creator in every sense of the word — writer, composer, inventor, and entrepreneur.

Before writing *How Not to F*cking Hate People*, he published *The 420 Gourmet: The Elevated Art of Cannabis Cuisine* (Harper Wave) under the name **JeffThe420Chef**, becoming one of the world's top ten award-winning cannabis chefs and the first to release a major-publisher cookbook. His pioneering work helped patients use cannabis to improve their quality of life and redefined the art of infused cuisine.

After COVID reshaped the world, Jeffrey pivoted from culinary innovation to human connection — exploring how people could heal not just their bodies, but their relationships, beliefs, and even their politics.

Today, he is the part owner of a small health-and-fitness shop in West Hollywood — affectionately known to locals as *Jeff's Bodega* — where daily conversations with hundreds of customers about love, loss, work, and even the world's most divisive debates inspired this book. Each exchange became raw material for one question: *How do we learn to respect each other and stay kind in a world built to make us hate each other?*

In everything he creates — food, music, or words — Jeffrey's mission is simple: make the world a little less cruel and a lot more human.

He's lived a full, messy, grateful life — one filled with reinvention, faith, heartbreak, fatherhood, and second chances. A proud gay dad and granddad, Jeffrey believes in God but not in the walls that divide people in His name. He lives by one simple mantra: kindness isn't weakness — it's wisdom. And it's always free.

"Without love, where would you be now?"

— *Tom Johnston,* **"Long Train Runnin'"** *(The Doobie Brothers, 1973)*

www.ingramcontent.com/pod-product-compliance
Lightning Source LLC
Chambersburg PA
CBHW052129030426
42337CB00028B/5085